the new Beetle vw

Jonathan Wood

the creation of a twenty first century classic

the new vw
Beetle

Jonathan Wood

CLB

CONTENTS

5136: The New Beetle
Published by Quadrillion Publishing Limited,
Godalming Business Centre, Woolsack Way, Godalming, GU7 1XW, UK
in association with Borders Press, a division of Borders Group, Inc.
100 Phoenix Drive, Ann Arbor, Michigan, 48108

Borders Press is a trademark of Borders Properties, Inc.

ISBN 0-6811-1396-0
Printed and bound in Spain

" IT WAS BOTH LOGICAL AND INEVITABLE THAT CONCEPT 1 SHOULD BE LAUNCHED IN AMERICA, ONCE VOLKSWAGEN'S LARGEST MARKET IN THE DAYS OF THE ORIGINAL BEETLE. **"**

FOREWORD

If historical precedent is anything to go by, the New Beetle is going to be around for a long time. After all, the original Beetle, the car that inspired it, was designed in the 1930s and entered production in 1945. Over fifty years later it is still being manufactured, having been sold in practically every country throughout the world. Now only built in Mexico and with over 21 million produced, it is the most popular car in the history of the automobile.

But one of the downsides of this extraordinary success is that Volkswagen, its manufacturer, left the car in production for too long in Germany and it was only the timely arrival, in 1974, of the wholly-unrelated front-wheel-drive Golf hatchback that saved the company.

It is for this reason that a Beetle revival could never have emerged from VW's Wolfsburg headquarters, because of the corporate trauma of the early 1970s when Germany's largest car-maker flirted with bankruptcy. In such circumstances, it could not have countenanced reviving the concept, even if the resulting car's mechanicals were unrelated to the original.

So the revival occurred some 7000 miles to the west, at Simi Valley, California, where in 1991 Volkswagen had established its first design studio outside the European continent. It is not without significance that Americans J Carroll Mays and Freeman Thomas, who co-designed Concept 1, the show car that paved the way to the New Beetle proper, were steeped in American and European styling influences, both having worked in the German motor industry before returning to the US.

Yet another all-important strand to the New Beetle story is the change in Volkswagen's management that occurred at the beginning of 1993, with the arrival of the dynamic Ferdinand Piëch as chairman. The grandson of Ferdinand Porsche, creator of the original Beetle, Piëch came to Wolfsburg from VW's Audi subsidiary, which is where the talented Mays also began his corporate career.

It was both logical and inevitable that Concept 1 should be launched in America, once Volkswagen's largest market in the days of the original Beetle. But by 1994 the era when it dominated US imports was long gone, and a revival spearheaded by the New Beetle had compelling corporate appeal.

There seems little doubt that Volkswagen was genuinely surprised by the enthusiastic response that greeted Concept 1's appearance at the beginning of 1994. It was a message confirmed by the company's own market research findings and, by the end of 1994, it had decided to put this previously unscheduled model into production.

The choice of Mexico to build the car was similarly sensible because of its proximity to America—potentially the New Beetle's largest market. Even more significantly, the car could be built at a highly competitive price because Mexican wage levels are much lower than in VW's European facilities.

The 1998 launch at Detroit's Auto Show, attended by chairman Piëch, was by any account a triumph. The press was ecstatic, the New Beetle emerged as Car of the Show, and ever since then Americans have been lining up to buy it. Europeans are already straining at the leash; their chance will come in 1999, and the rest of the world beckons.

Of course there are corporate fears that this could be a temporary sales phenomenon, but it seems unlikely. The Beetle's shape is so deeply etched into the post-war world's collective psyche that it produces an instant and favorable response in potential purchasers.

In short, customers are buying a model steeped in nostalgia but without the shortcomings of the original, because beneath those beckoning curves are the proven, ultra-reliable mechanicals of Volkswagen's latest Golf. With such a parentage the New Beetle's future looks bright indeed!

1991 Volkswagen opens a Design Center at the Simi Valley Business Center, California, USA, its first non-European design studio. It is headed by J. Carroll Mays, who joined the company in 1980

January 1993 Ferdinand Piëch, formerly chairman of VW's Audi subsidiary, is appointed chairman of the board of management of Volkswagen AG. He is the grandson of Ferdinand Porsche, designer of the Volkswagen Beetle

1993 Mays and fellow stylist, design manager Freeman Thomas, begin work at Simi Valley on Concept 1, inspired by the original Beetle sedan

January 5th 1994 Concept 1 is unveiled to the press at the North American Auto Show, Detroit. It goes on to receive universal acclaim and Volkswagen of America will receive some 35,000 appreciative letters and phone calls throughout the year and into 1995

November 1994 Volkswagen decides to manufacture Concept 1 before the turn of the millennium. A team of engineers, under design director Hartmut Warkuss, begins work on transforming Mays' concept car into a production reality

A CHRONOLOGY 1991–1998

March 8th 1994 The Cabriolet version of Concept 1 is displayed at the Geneva Motor Show. Ferdinand Piëch hints that Volkswagen may put both versions into production

October 25th 1995 Concept 1, as revised by Wolfsburg, is displayed at the Tokyo Motor Show. An enlarged version of Mays' original, it is based on Volkswagen's A-class platform created for the Mark IV Golf that is due to enter production in 1997

May 1997 Volkswagen unveils official photographs of the New Beetle, which inherits all the visual appeal of Concept 1. Wolfsburg's cosmetic contribution includes the presence of a dashboard mounted bud vase, which revives memories of the 1950s and '60s. The car is to be built at Volkswagen's factory at Puebla, Mexico

March 1996 Concept 1 is renamed the New Beetle at the Geneva Motor Show. It is fitted with Volkswagen's proven 1.9 liter TDI turbo diesel engine, one of two power units that will initially be on offer

October 1997 The Mark IV version of Volkswagen's best-selling Golf, since 1983 Europe's most popular car, is announced. The New Beetle will share its platform and mechanical components

January 5th 1998 Ferdinand Piëch launches the model at the North American Auto Show and it features in New Beetle World, Volkswagen's largest ever exhibit at the event. The motoring press judges it Car of the Show

February 24th 1998 American motoring journalists are the first in the world to have an opportunity to drive the New Beetle at Atlanta, Georgia

March 1998 Sales of the New Beetle begin in North America with a 50,000 first year target, soon upped to 65,000

October 1998 The New Beetle's European launch is staged at the Paris Motor Show. Right-hand-drive cars, for the British and Japanese markets, are destined for mid-1999

CHAPTER
1 A CONCEPT EVOLVES

" WE WANTED TO VISUALIZE VOLKSWAGEN'S TRADITIONAL QUALITIES OF HONESTY, SIMPLICITY, RELIABILITY, AND ORIGINALITY. **"** J. CARROLL MAYS, CO-DESIGNER OF CONCEPT 1

IT LOOKS LIKE nothing else, apart from its legendary predecessor. The New Beetle is off-beat, its styling a skilful synthesis of past and present themes, and its unashamed inspiration is the most successful car in the history of the automobile. And while the original Beetle has dominated the world's highways in the second half of the 20th century, the New Beetle is spearheading a revitalized, expansionist Volkswagen into the 21st.

What's more, this VW usually produces smiles on the faces of those who encounter it. Not many cars can achieve that.

Unveiled at the 1998 Detroit Auto Show, the model first went on sale in the United States, with Europe following in the fall and the rest of the world in 1999. This makes the New Beetle a true world car, just like its famous forebear. For the time being the original Beetle remains in production; it was at VW's Mexican factory that the 21 millionth came off the line, which is where the new car is also being assembled.

While the original Beetle is powered by a noisy, air cooled, rear mounted engine, the latter day version benefits from the

A NEW LEGEND IS BORN

American origins: computer-assisted design of a roadwheel for Concept 1 being evaluated at Volkswagen's Simi Valley Design Center. In the event a wheel with six rather than five spokes was adopted for the production version

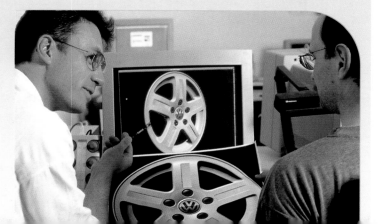

mechanical underpinnings of VW's latest front-wheel-drive Golf that is Europe's most popular car.

US AND GERMANY WORK TOGETHER

The model's global profile is further underlined by the fact that this car is the product of a US/German alliance, initiated in 1991. That year Volkswagen opened its Design Center in Simi Valley, California. Such US facilities are now commonplace amongst the industry's Big Battalions and are a recognition of America as the world's largest and most lucrative motoring marketplace.

The Volkswagen executive charged with the task of establishing this West Coast facility was 36 year old J Carroll Mays, who began his corporate career in 1980 with the in-house Audi concern based in Germany.

Motor cars are in Mays' blood. He grew up near Oklahoma City, where his retired rancher father ran a modest chain of autoparts stores. Young Mays soon displayed a talent for drawing cars, although he initially majored in journalism at the University of Oklahoma. But his precocious artistic abilities got the better of him and he subsequently moved to the Art Center College of Design in Pasadena, graduating in 1980.

That year Mays crossed the Atlantic, having secured a job as an exterior designer with Audi at Ingolstadt. An arm of the mighty Volkswagen company since 1965, it was headed by Ferdinand Piëch (born 1937), who had been appointed chairman in 1988.

Piëch is the grandson of the redoubtable Ferdinand Porsche, after whom he was named, his mother Louise having been the great Austrian engineer's daughter. The Stuttgart-based Porsche bureau was responsible for the Volkswagen, initiated by Adolf Hitler in 1934, the design of which was completed in 1938.

THE GOLF SUCCEEDS THE BEETLE

In 1972 Audi had introduced the influential 80 sedan, the first of a new generation of front-wheel-drive models, and in 1973 came a Volkswagen Passat derivative. The child proved to be the savior of the parent because the Audi-related Volkswagen Golf of 1974 was destined to be the true successor of the Beetle. The popularity of the Wolfsburg firm's mainstay had, at long last, begun to wane.

Overall responsibility for the 80 was vested in Hartmut Warkuss (born 1940), who had begun his career with Mercedes-Benz and joined Audi in 1968 from Ford at Cologne. In 1976 he was put in charge of Audi design and it was Warkuss to whom the 25 year old Mays reported. A brief spell with BMW apart, the

Above

J. Carroll Mays, co-designer of Concept 1. He returned to Germany in 1993 to take over Audi's worldwide design but left late in 1994. In 1997 he became vice president of Ford's design operations

Right

Concept 1 pictured outside the Design Center, opened in 1991. This facility allows VW to study the styling influences of the US market. In addition to Mays and Freeman Thomas, the team responsible for the car was Charles Ellwood, H. Michael Tozer, John Bandringa, Steve Anderson, Franz von Holzhausen, Marc Florian, and Derek Jenkins, working alongside a group of eight sculptors

Volkswagen's imposing Wolfsburg factory, still the largest car plant in the world under one roof. The original Beetle was built there between 1940 and 1974. The power station supplies both the works and the adjoining town of Wolfsburg. In the foreground is the Mittelland Canal

California, where Simi Valley is located, has some of the most rigorous emissions standards in the world. In 1992, against this background, Mays and Thomas began work on an environmentally friendly electrically powered concept car that marks the starting point of the New Beetle project. But as Mays later told the British *Autocar* magazine: "Nobody wants to drive electric cars that look like electric cars."

He recognized that such advanced technology required a stylistically acceptable package. In short, people had to be comfortable with it, and "if it was to be a VW, then no car was more comfortable than a Beetle."

As a result he drew up the specification of a Beetle-inspired design that he then submitted to Warkuss, his old boss at Audi.

THE VOLKSWAGEN EMPIRE GROWS

But there were changes taking place in the Volkswagen empire. It had been growing by acquisition; the purchase of Seat, Fiat's former Spanish subsidiary, was completed in 1986, and in 1991 VW bought the Czech Skoda concern.

Carl Hahn, chairman of the VW board since 1982, was due for retirement and he was replaced by Audi's Ferdinand Piëch, who took over the running of Europe's largest car maker in January 1993. From Ingolstadt he brought with him Hartmut Warkuss, who became corporate head of design.

Mays was given approval to proceed and then "we thought about what makes a Volkswagen and defined the values as simple, reliable, honest, and truthful."

Stylistic inspiration was to be provided by the presence of a 1946 Beetle, owned by enthusiast Johnny von Neumann, a product of the era when VW operated under British army occupation.

young American set up Audi's advanced styling studio in Munich in conjunction with British stylist Martin Smith, who later enjoyed a distinguished career with the General Motors-owned Opel concern.

The outcome of this impressive concentration of talent was the Audi Avus concept car that appeared at the 1991 Tokyo Motor Show. The idea was to out-Japanese the Japanese, and the sleek, gleaming coupé, with four-wheel-drive, a V12 mid-engine, aluminum body, large 20in (508mm) wheels, and a distinctive glazed cockpit, did precisely that.

But by this time Mays was back in his native America. He had left Germany in 1989 and went on to open Volkswagen of America's Design Center. The nine years that Mays spent in Europe would stand him in good stead and he regarded his two Audi colleagues, Warkuss and Smith, as his formative stylistic gurus.

PLANNING NEW CARS IN SIMI VALLEY

Mays' assistant at Simi Valley was a fellow countryman who had a remarkably similar background to his own. Freeman Thomas is also a graduate of Pasadena's design college. Like Mays, he had crossed the Atlantic to gain experience of the European motor industry and similarly gravitated to Germany. But once there Thomas joined the world famous Porsche company.

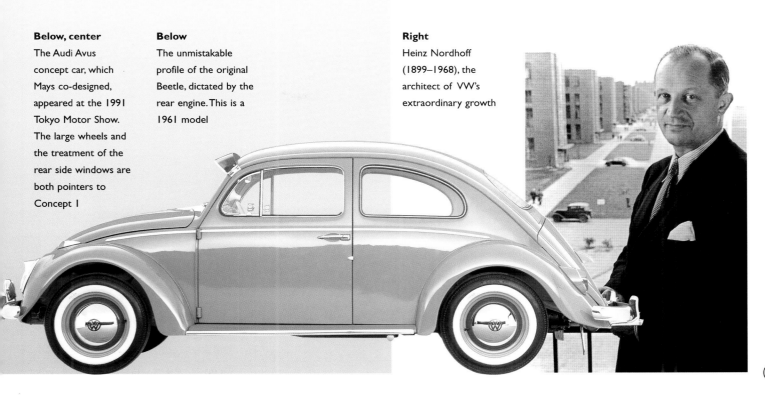

Below, center

The Audi Avus concept car, which Mays co-designed, appeared at the 1991 Tokyo Motor Show. The large wheels and the treatment of the rear side windows are both pointers to Concept 1

Below

The unmistakable profile of the original Beetle, dictated by the rear engine. This is a 1961 model

Right

Heinz Nordhoff (1899–1968), the architect of VW's extraordinary growth

BAUHAUS INFLUENCES

Both Mays and Thomas are ardent apostles of the 1920s Bauhaus school of design. Established in Germany, its global influence, with its emphasis on geometrical forms, resulted in mass produced artifacts benefiting from designs of a quality usually reserved for more expensive hand crafted items.

Each designer undertook the creation of a quarter-scale model with Mays' work reflecting a modern interpretation of the Beetle theme. Thomas' version, by contrast, embodied more nostalgic, so-called "retro" elements.

As the concept evolved, the duo began to look upon themselves as custodians of the creed laid down by Volkswagen's legendary general manager, Heinz Nordhoff. On taking over the VW plant in 1949, he had declared that the original Beetle should evolve organically, from the inside outward. The car could consequently be improved over the years without sacrificing its distinctive appearance. The New Beetle has therefore been conceived with this approach in mind.

Mays readily acknowledges that "the shape kept coming back to the Beetle" and, as the design progressed, Warkuss positively responded to the results. Interestingly, there were elements of Smith/Mays' Audi Avus in its albeit shorter and taller rear side windows. The prototype was based on the Seat Ibiza platform, courtesy of the yet unseen 1995 Volkswagen Polo.

As the project evolved the distinctive curvilinear elements of the original, as far as the roof and fenders were concerned, became readily apparent. Essentially steel bodied and yellow painted, the front and rear bumper areas were made of a deformable plastic material. Echoes of the Beetle were easily

identifiable in the detail design. The round headlamps, set back sloping in the fenders, were a case in point, along with adjacent twin oval grilles that mimicked the horn apertures of the original.

A NEW FACE

The idea was that the car should have a "face" and could be easily identified as a Volkswagen, even when the famous VW monogram was removed from its nose. And there were no air cooling intakes for the intended front mounted engine, just like the Beetle, which hadn't needed them anyway. The car's projected electrical power source wouldn't need them either, but they were a requirement of a conventional gas or diesel engine.

Unlike the original two-door sedan, the vehicle evolving in the California studio was to be a three-door hatchback. This was not immediately obvious as the hatch followed the contours of the body lines.

Above
In the United States, in the 1960s, Volkswagen produced scale models of its proposed sales outlets. The aim was to attain a corporate look. The advert dates from 1955, and was the work of VW's distributor for an area to the west of the Mississippi

Mechanically the new car was a world away from the original and, even though it was to be front engined, small grilles were introduced on the rear deck to suggest the presence of a power unit. However, this feature was firmly vetoed by chairman Piëch when he inspected the vehicle. A version of the design with a trunk was, incidentally, contemplated but then dispensed with.

Daringly, the rear of the car closely mirrored its front. The shape and stance of the taillamps were also the same as the headlamps, apart from the color of the lenses. Similarly the VW badge, which concealed the hatchlock, had its equivalent on the hood.

The interior was no less radical. The yellow metalwork was perpetuated inside while the steering wheel, instrument pod, and trim were finished in black. The dominant speedometer was located directly in front of the driver and evoked memories of the original.

For night driving, the dial was illuminated with an electro-luminescent green light and its introduction followed a photographic session with the car around the swimming pool at Mays' house. Just think about the color of chlorine-laced pool water. . . .

" BY THIS TIME WHAT EUROPEANS CALLED THE BEETLE...HAD ETCHED ITSELF DEEPLY INTO THE AMERICAN AUTOMOTIVE PSYCHE. "

Left

A sketch of Concept 1, as refined by Wolfsburg, with engine cooling grilles and sliding roof, features that were revealed at the 1995 Tokyo Motor Show. But the three spoke wheels did not reach production

There was provision for air conditioning to be fitted, and as a result the air outlets featured in the highly distinctive black hued central console.

But again you were never far away from the Beetle proper. The passenger grab handle was a reminder of past Wolfsburg practice, the durable carpeting was similarly inspired and the sills were a modern, aerodynamically honed interpretation of the original Beetle's vestigial running boards.

At 59in (1500mm) the car's height was the same as its predecessor's, and allowed Mays to raise the seats by some 5.9in (150mm) in comparison with other mainstream VW products. They were also moved further forward to allow more room for the rear passengers, although this accommodation remained somewhat limited.

In overall terms, the vehicle was both longer, at 150.5in (3824mm), and wider, at 64in (1636mm), than the definitive Beetle.

the briefest of smiles....Mays was thus given the corporate approval to proceed.

With its debut destined for the 1994 Detroit Motor Show, on January 5th, Volkswagen would be keenly gauging the public response to what was still regarded as a concept car. However, director of research Ulrich Seiffert sounded a note of caution when he declared that there were no "concrete plans" to put Concept 1 into production even though the company urgently needed to do so.

Volkswagen had never been able to repeat the success of the original Beetle on the American market. Sales had officially begun there in 1949 with Nordhoff's enhanced and ultimately ultra reliable Export model. But it was not until 1955 that it moved ahead to become America's largest selling imported car.

An impressive dealer network and an excellent spares service was buttressed by an inspired advertising campaign, "I don't want an imported car, I want a Volkswagen." Annual sales soared, peaking in 1968 at 423,008. But in 1975 the Beetle ceded its pole position to the Japanese Toyota Corolla.

Its 18in (457mm) wheels were also larger, six-spoked and 2in (50mm) wider than the originals. Again, the precedent of the Avus concept car is apparent.

In its original manifestation this experimental Volkswagen was to be electrically powered and two versions, one using sodium nickel batteries and the other, a diesel/electric hybrid, were mentioned as possible power sources.

But a conventional engine would also be required and the obvious power unit was the Golf's 1.9 liter turbocharged diesel. American sales could also be enhanced by the option of Volkswagen's Ecomatic automatic transmission introduced on the Golf in 1993.

In Simi Valley, much of that year had been spent working on what had been named Concept 1, so called because it echoed the Type 1 designation of the original Beetle.

MAKING ASSESSMENTS IN VALHALLA

The final decision to display the car publicly lay with Volkswagen's chairman and the prototype was transported to Germany for his approval. The viewing was at a place the company called Valhalla, the mythological hall of the Norse gods. It was also where Nordhoff used to sanction the latest improvements to the original Beetle range.

As Thomas later told *Automobile* magazine, "Dr Piëch and his entourage came in for a very private viewing. . . .He looked at the car and said '*In Ordnung*,' which is a very cold way of saying 'In Order'." And the usually taciturn Piëch even allowed himself

Above
Concept 1's speedometer already showing the distinctive green lighting used in the production car

Below and right
Concept 1, as it appeared in 1994, with its inspiration from the original Beetle very apparent

By this time what Europeans called the Beetle—it was "the Bug" in the States—had etched itself deeply into the American automotive psyche. From becoming a popular and classless second family car, the rattling chuff-chuff of its seemingly unburstable air cooled, rear mounted engine was soon being heard in increasing numbers around the country's university campuses.

But later the model was withdrawn from the US market, imports having ceased in 1977, to be replaced by the Golf, marketed in the US as the Rabbit. Although this front-wheel-drive hatchback was destined to become Europe's most popular car, the heavily Americanized Rabbit, built at the Westmoreland plant, was not appreciated by Americans, who wanted to buy a "German" car. As a result it never attained the success of the Beetle there, and Westmoreland was closed down. The Golf is now imported from the Mexican factory at Puebla. Since VW's Brazilian plant ceased production of the Beetle in 1996, Puebla has been the sole source of the model. In 1988 Volkswagen sold some 168,000 units in the US, but by 1993 sales had slumped to about 50,000 and a prototype small car designed in Wolfsburg and named the Chico had been expensively cancelled at the eleventh hour. The Beetle-inspired Concept 1, which drew deeply on American reserves of good faith for the model, had not arrived a moment too soon.

CONCEPT 1 SUCCEEDS AT THE 1994 DETROIT MOTOR SHOW

To the company's delight it was able to describe the response to the car at the Detroit show as "phenomenal." Mays declared that "there were just two cars in Detroit that everyone would recognize if you took the badges off: Concept 1 and the [Porsche] 911."

WOB ⊕ 1994

Volkswagen of America issued a brochure at the show that expanded on Mays' pithy four-word design philosophy. It was a message perpetuated in a promotional video distributed to the company's dealer network.

By the time the '94 Detroit show closed its doors on January 16th, Volkswagen, although encouraged by the response, was still noncommittal about Concept 1's future. A corporate press statement declared that "the decision as to whether it will be put into full scale production has yet to be made."

A telephone line was subsequently set up by Volkswagen of America and there was universal public approval for the reappearance of what many members of the population regarded as the return of an old friend. And, most significantly, more customers began to visit VW showrooms to provide the firm with its best monthly sales totals since 1990. The omens looked good.

This sea change in US public opinion was neatly summed up by Professor Seiffert when he was asked whether the modern generation of Americans would respond to a car that was in its heyday before they were born.

That, he maintained, would make no difference. "The father will tell them; the mother will tell them, the mother in law will tell them." He had spoken with young Americans and they "want to know why they too can't have it today."

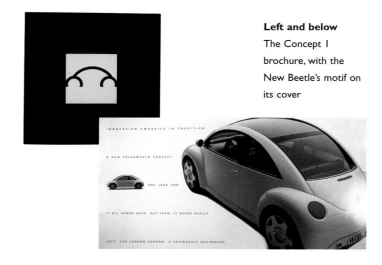

Left and below
The Concept 1 brochure, with the New Beetle's motif on its cover

Below
Concept 1 as it appeared at the 1994 Detroit show. It was what VW described as a "back to the future concept" and succeeded in producing an enthusiastic response from members of the public at the event

Below

Although there was plenty of room in the front of Concept 1, there would be even more in the New Beetle because of the Golf Mk IV platform

Above

The instrument panel and center console clearly relate to the production version

Left

The door handle with its press-open button and accompanying recess is one of the many design cues on Concept 1 that echoed the original Beetle. The uncompromising vertical door line is another inheritance

Above

Concept 1 had large 18 inch diameter wheels, which were reduced by two inches by the time they reached the production line. The front wheels are driven, unlike those of the original Beetle

A CONCEPT 1 CABRIOLET FOR THE SWISS

But would Detroit's response to Concept 1 be repeated in Europe? The first major event of the year was the Geneva Motor Show, which opened its doors to the press on March 8th, a mere seven weeks after the closure of the American display.

By this time Mays had returned to Europe and Audi, where he replaced Hartmut Warkuss as design director. At Geneva a cabriolet version of Concept 1 made its appearance, the work of British designer Charles Ellwood, who had been a member of the team that created the original car. The open version was built in the brief gap that occurred between the two shows.

Because of this rapid gestation, Volkswagen's chairman, Ferdinand Piëch, saw the open version of Concept 1 for the first time at Geneva. There he was able to give the strongest indication yet that Volkswagen was contemplating building the car.

He declared to an audience at the show: "We at Volkswagen do not intend visions to remain visions. We want them to become reality." He then added, significantly, "This is equally true of the Concept 1 and the Concept 1 Cabriolet."

Two months later, in May, news broke that Piëch wanted to study where the production version of Concept 1 might be built.

THE NEW CAR IS GIVEN THE GO AHEAD

It would not be until November of 1994 that the project was finally given the corporate green light, and followed positive findings from market research in America, which was its intended principal market. Volkswagen declared that "successful research and development of Concept 1 has given us no option but to build the car before the end of the decade."

The chosen factory was the Mexican plant, which was to produce 100,000 units a year, to go on sale in the US in 1998.

The project was then handed over to Volkswagen's Wolfsburg factory with a brief to turn the Mays/Thomas dream into a production reality. The engineering team was working under the direction of Hartmut Warkuss, who, appropriately, had sanctioned the Concept 1 program in the first place.

The initial results of their labors were displayed at the 1995 Tokyo Motor Show in the form of a revised version of Concept 1. At the press day, held on October 25th, Ferdinand Piëch declared: "When we first presented the Concept 1 at the 1994 Detroit Motor Show we were overwhelmed by the positive response. Since then we have talked to customers and dealers all over the world, and taken careful note of the recommendations of the media and motoring press. Why? Because we want to put a car on the markets of the world that perfectly corresponds to the requirements, desires, and dreams of our customers.

"Today we invite you to acquaint yourselves with the current status of Concept 1. Look at the car and when doing so bear in mind that the memories of yesterday can also form the basis of the dream of tomorrow."

The revised Concept 1, finished in gleaming black, reflected some significant changes to the original while not sacrificing its strong visual appeal. External revisions particularly related to the car's front end. It now had integral body colored bumpers and, more significantly, engine cooling vents beneath them. A casualty was the original's Beetle-inspired small circular grilles, while new enlarged circular headlamps replaced the originals.

A THIRD CONCEPT 1 APPEARS

Most importantly, the Tokyo version of Concept 1 featured a new platform, one that had been developed for the Volkswagen Golf Mark IV. In fact, it first appeared on the Audi 3 hatchback, launched in 1996, and the new Golf did not get it until 1997. It was both longer, at 159 in (4060mm), and wider, at 2.7in (70mm), than the versions shown at Detroit and Geneva in the previous year.

Inside, the seats were upholstered in light colored leather, although the essentials of the original Mays/Thomas design were retained. Yet a further variation was the introduction of a sunroof, which appeared black on the outside, although the occupants would have an uninterrupted view of the sky.

A car featuring the Tokyo revisions made an appearance at the 1996 Geneva Motor Show. There what the company described as a "pearlescent cyber green" two door sedan ceased to be Concept 1 when Volkswagen announced that the car was to be called the New Beetle. It was badged as such although specifications and trim variants were still undecided. A new feature was a Porsche-designed sliding roof as featured on the 1996 Porsche Targa 911.

At this stage three engines would be offered. The Geneva show car was fitted with the Golf's 1.9 liter direct injection turbocharged diesel, and Volkswagen announced that two gasoline engines, respectively developing 105 and 150 bhp, would also be made available.

For the next 14 months information on the New Beetle proved tantalizingly scarce until Volkswagen revealed further details of the model in May 1997, indicating that it would be unveiled at the 1998 Detroit Motor Show.

News of the cabriolet

Intriguingly, too, came more definite news of the cabriolet version. But, unlike the original, which was produced by Karmann in Germany, it would also hail from Volkswagen's Mexican plant, although it was unlikely to appear until the 2000 season.

In December 1997, with the January 1998 launch looming, Volkswagen unveiled more pictures of the definitive version that had already entered production in Puebla. The plant had been equipped with the latest laser welding technology to ensure a consistent build quality of the new car's body. As recounted in Chapter Four, the Detroit launch proved a triumph for Volkswagen and its New Beetle. In the meantime, let's take a closer look beneath the surface of this remarkable car.

The open version of Concept 1 was the work of Charles Ellwood, who currently runs Volkswagen's Simi Valley Design Center

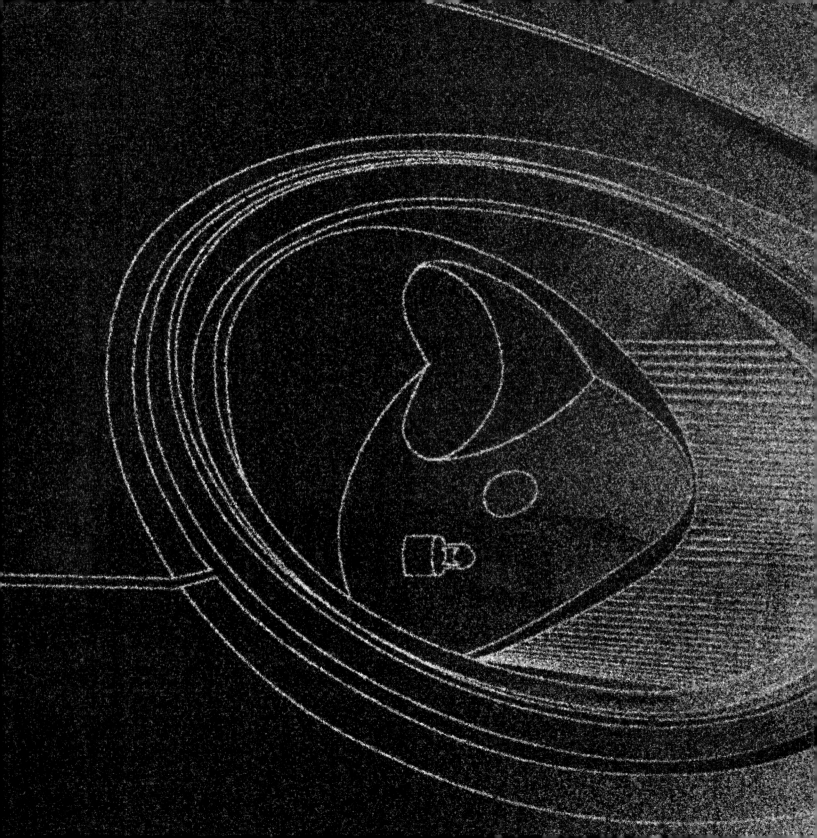

CHAPTER

2 STYLING, INSIDE & OUT

"WE AT VOLKSWAGEN DO NOT INTEND VISIONS TO REMAIN VISIONS. WE WANT THEM TO BECOME REALITY."

FERDINAND PIËCH, CHAIRMAN, VOLKSWAGEN AG

THERE CAN BE LITTLE DOUBT that Wolfsburg's transformation of Concept 1 into the New Beetle has been skilfully and sensitively accomplished. What Volkswagen has done is produce a car with all the visual appeal of the original Beetle but none of its vices.

THE HERITAGE

Not only is this 1998 VW far faster, more comfortable and quieter than its predecessor, its front-wheel-drive mechanicals are well proven, as millions of satisfied Golf customers can testify.

But the car looks as it does because, in spirit, it echoes the original, a point underlined by Volkswagen's chairman, Ferdinand Piëch, at the 1998 launch to the world's motoring press.

There he maintained that "The New Beetle cannot deny its origins and the magic of its shape." So what are these "origins"? To discover its roots and why this car looks as it does, it is necessary to retrace our steps to Germany of the 1930s. But what also emerges is that the New Beetle's Teutonic/American roots are wholly in keeping with the origins and extraordinary evolution of the car that inspired it.

THE ORIGINS OF THE BEETLE

When Adolf Hitler became German Chancellor in January 1933, one of his first actions was to initiate the autobahn program. These purpose-built roads had been pioneered by Mussolini, his fascist counterpart in Italy, and by 1943 there were some 2000 miles of concrete freeways spread across Germany.

The second strand of Hitler's automotive strategy was that the Nazi state would initiate the mass production of a small car. He hoped that it would be built by the German motor industry and be sufficiently inexpensive to be within reach of the average German who would never otherwise have been able to contemplate car ownership.

His inspiration was Henry Ford's "Tin Lizzie," the Model T Ford, and the German leader had read this American hero's autobiography, *My Life and Work*, while imprisoned in Landsberg Castle in 1924. The tough, value-for-money Ford was the world's first truly mass-produced car, and was at the time by far the most popular vehicle in the history of the automobile.

By 1919 it was estimated that every other car in the world was a go-anywhere Model T. By the time production ceased in 1927, some 15 million had been built since the start of manufacture in 1908.

Above left
Ferdinand Porsche (second left) points out details of the new KdF-Wagen to Adolf Hitler, who conceived the idea of a German People's Car

Above and right
The Beetle as it entered production after the war. This example dates from 1948, when the factory was run by the British army. The distinctive split rear window was discontinued in 1953

TALKS WITH PORSCHE

Early in 1934 Hitler began talks with the famous Austrian engineer, Ferdinand Porsche, about his thoughts for a car that could be sold for under RM (Reichsmark) 1000 ($142). Although Porsche had worked for some of Europe's most famous car companies, he had built his reputation as technical director of Mercedes-Benz. In the depression year of 1930 he had decided to leave the industry and open his own Stuttgart-based design bureau.

His apprehensions were considerable but he had little choice other than to accept the commission for a German People's Car, or Volkswagen, and was given a mere 10 months to complete the work. But the task proved to be considerably more difficult than he envisaged, and the design was not finished until 1938. This was mainly because of the problem the engineering team experienced in finding a cheap and efficient engine. Hitler had also stipulated an air cooled engine, because of its low cost. Eventually, a rear mounted horizontally opposed four cylinder unit was adopted.

The finished car was available in two guises. The oh-so-basic version cost RM 990 ($141) and, like the Model T that for a time could only be ordered in black, was solely available in blue-gray livery. An extra RM 60 ($8) would buy a folding cloth sunroof.

The car, styled by the bureau's Erwin Komenda, looked as it did for a variety of reasons, the essentials of which are inherited by the New Beetle. Its shape was mainly influenced by the fact that it had a rear engine, because that is the cheapest place to locate a vehicle's power unit.

As it happened Porsche had already designed what proved to be a stillborn two door rear engined saloon for motorcycle manufacturer NSU. So when the Stuttgart team began work on the German People's Car, it was based on this existing design.

"TWO ADULTS AND THREE CHILDREN"

The projected VW therefore had a similarly frugal body style with space inside for two adults and three children. This requirement was also set down in Porsche's design brief and similarly emanated from the German Chancellor.

> **" IT SHOULD LOOK LIKE A BEETLE. YOU'VE ONLY GOT TO LOOK TO NATURE TO FIND OUT WHAT STREAMLINING IS. "**

Adolf Hitler was, incidentally, also responsible for likening the car to a beetle. On one memorable occasion he declared: "It should look like a beetle. You've only got to look to nature to find out what streamlining is." To save money the experimental versions were bereft of a rear window, or indeed cooling louvers on the engine cover. Consequently, these pre-production cars looked very beetle-like!

An unexpected technological benefit of the growth of the German autobahn network was that it stimulated research into the science of aerodynamics. On a straight road, a "slippery" car that passes easily through the air benefits both in performance and fuel consumption.

The highly curvaceous "streamlined" Volkswagen was typical of many wind cheating designs of the day that were in striking contrast to their elegant but angular counterparts of the previous decade.

Theoretically a rear powered car possesses a better drag coefficient than a front engined one because there is no intrusive vertically positioned radiator to interrupt the air flow. For the same

Two KdF-Wagens (these are Daimler-Benz built pre-production versions) present for the laying of the factory's foundation stone by Hitler in May 1938. The saloon entered limited production in 1940 but the cabriolet (open) version did not appear until 1949

reason, the shape of the hood is not dictated by the presence of an engine. The Volkswagen scored on these fronts and, for the same reasons, very progressively for its time, the headlamps were faired into the front fenders. Those on the New Beetle are similarly positioned, although this practice has, of course, long since been commonplace. However, back in the 1930s such lights were often left free standing.

Models of the German People's Car were duly wind tunnel tested. Although the finished product does look remarkably "slippery" from an aerodynamic standpoint, its original drag coefficient of 0.48 is not particularly good. This is a reflection of the fact that, in the main, its looks overrode any wind cheating considerations, a dilemma that still faces car stylists the world over as they endeavor to reconcile these twin demands. The truly aerodynamic car often appears bizarre and is thus unmarketable. For the record, the New Beetle's drag coefficient is a much more respectable 0.38.

It was not until 1938 that Hitler decreed that the state would manufacture the car. It was also the year in which the Volkswagen was renamed the KdF-Wagen, the Nazi's 'Strength through Joy' (Kraft durch Freude) car.

Work also began on a greenfield site, some 50 miles from Hanover in the north of Germany, on a purpose designed factory in which to mass produce the model in hitherto unimaginable quantities. The adjoining community built to house the plant's

In part the Beetle looked as it did because it reflected the "streamlined" look of the 1930s and had been aerodynamically tested. This 1975 example is pictured in the Volkswagen wind tunnel and by this time its Cd (drag coefficient) was not particularly impressive at 0.44

workforce was accordingly named KdF-Stadt, town of the Strength through Joy car.

Once again the Ford influence is apparent because the factory, located alongside the Mittelland Canal, was inspired by Henry Ford's mighty Rouge River factory in Detroit. Porsche headed a small team that visited America in 1936 and 1937 to recruit German nationals to work in the new plant.

As will have become apparent, from the outset the car was designed specifically for the German market. But to maintain the volumes envisaged—a staggering 1.5 million cars per annum were planned by 1942—overseas sales were essential. This figure was far in excess of any European totals and would have rivalled the Titans of Detroit.

A CAR FOR THE FAVORED FEW

But the outbreak in 1939 of the Second World War meant that the KdF-Wagen never reached the German public. Production began in 1940 and only some 600 or so cars were built, which mostly went to the higher echelons of the Nazi party.

With the ending of hostilities the war-ravaged KdF-Wagen factory fell within the British military zone. The British army occupied the factory and, at the end of 1945, production restarted and the car once again reverted to the Volkswagen name.

Similarly the adjoining town became Wolfsburg, having taken its name from the nearby medieval castle, the factory having been built on part of what had once been its estate. A representation of the fortress also became the Volkswagen's badge.

VOLKSWAGEN'S FIRST POSTWAR MANAGER

The VW works remained under British occupation until 1949, when it was handed back to the German state. In the previous year the military authorities had appointed 48 year old Heinz Nordhoff as Volkswagen's general manager. A former director of the General Motors-owned Opel concern, he had visited America before the war and was well acquainted with transatlantic mass production methods and the potential of its market.

Firmly in control, Nordhoff took two inspired decisions that were destined to make the Volkswagen the most popular car in the history of the automobile. Firstly, he decided that Wolfsburg would make the car in one engine capacity, a philosophy that held firm until the 1960s. In this approach there were clear echoes of Henry Ford's one model policy.

Secondly, although Nordhoff was the first to recognize that the noisy, badly built sedan had numerous faults, he was well aware of the fact "that Professor Porsche had worked something into it that made this diamond well worth our while polishing."

Left
Heinz Nordhoff at a Beetle-populated Wolfsburg. This was one of a series of photos planned for the front cover of *Time* magazine

Right
Concept 1, as revised by Wolfsburg, was noticeably larger than the original because it was based on the Golf Mk IV platform. The sliding roof introduced on this car was enhanced by its black paintwork

Below
The side mirrors followed the '94 Detroit show car

Below
The principal visual difference between the front of the revised German version of Concept 1 and the original was the introduction of the air intake, required by the presence of a gas or diesel engine, integral bumpers and much improved headlamps

29

STYLING, INSIDE AND OUT

Open wide! The raised trunk lid reveals the extent of curvature introduced into the substantial rear window. The horizontal lines on the fenders mark the start of the deformable plastic bumpers

Right
Luggage can be easily loaded because of the large trunk lid and the low sill

For all these reasons the Beetle has made its indelible mark on the world and this is the New Beetle's pedigree. Most significantly, it has inherited elements of its predecessor's unique appearance, although it is not a visual pastiche of the original.

It was a point underlined by Martin Winterkorn, Volkswagen's head of technical development, at the car's launch. There he revealed the enthusiasm exhibited by Americans for the model, even before it had reached production.

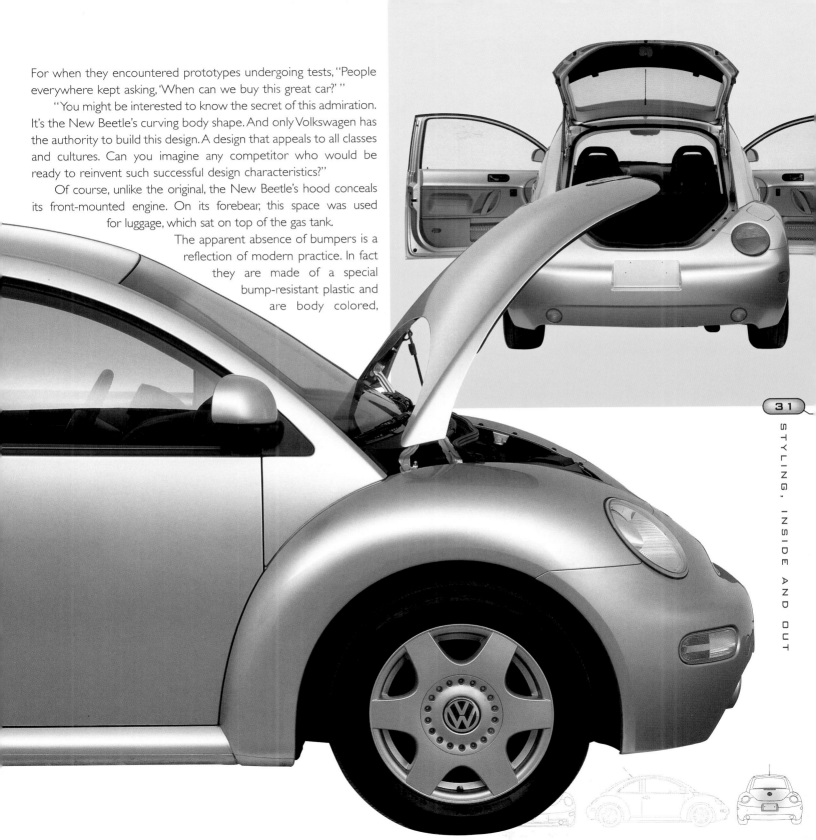

For when they encountered prototypes undergoing tests, "People everywhere kept asking, 'When can we buy this great car?' "

"You might be interested to know the secret of this admiration. It's the New Beetle's curving body shape. And only Volkswagen has the authority to build this design. A design that appeals to all classes and cultures. Can you imagine any competitor who would be ready to reinvent such successful design characteristics?"

Of course, unlike the original, the New Beetle's hood conceals its front-mounted engine. On its forebear, this space was used for luggage, which sat on top of the gas tank.

The apparent absence of bumpers is a reflection of modern practice. In fact they are made of a special bump-resistant plastic and are body colored,

along with the electrically heated side mirror housings and door handles.

However, the principal structural difference is that while the original had only two doors, the New Beetle is a hatchback. There was no question of the first Volkswagen having been so. Apart from the rear-mounted engine, the three- or five-door configuration did not gain popularity until the 1970s.

A LASER WELDED BODY

The New Beetle's body is fully galvanized with a 12 year rust through and corrosion warranty and is the result of a 26-step paint/corrosion process. The shell also benefits from the latest laser welding technology, which produces a body with a remarkably high static and torsional stiffness.

It has therefore permitted, said Dr Winterkorn, "very small gaps in external sheet metal welds" to the benefit of both driving and handling. "It might even remind you of the first time you ever drove

> " UNLIKE THE ORIGINAL, THE NEW BEETLE'S HOOD CONCEALS A FRONT-MOUNTED ENGINE. ON ITS FOREBEAR THE SPACE BENEATH WAS USED FOR LUGGAGE.... "

Left
For safety reasons, the New Beetle is fitted with daylight running lights. Once the car is started, they operate on reduced power

Below

Although the engine is at the front, unlike the original, the front of the New Beetle succeeds in perpetuating that distinctive Beetle look. The headlamps have halogen projector beams while low mounted front fog lamps are optional

Right

The shape of the taillights echoes that of the headlights. Note the high level stop lamp on the trunk lid below the rear window and above the VW badge. An electric rear window defroster is standard, as is tinted glass

STYLING, INSIDE AND OUT

a go-kart round the track." The aerodynamics also benefit and, in turn, wind noise is reduced.

The headlights, which clearly reflected those of the original, were "another brilliant detail. The innovative technology of the high-tech [halogen] projector beams can be seen behind the crystal clear polycarbonate lenses." Fog lamps of a similar specification are available as part of an optional sport package, and are positioned below the front bumper.

The taillights, in location and shape, echo the headlamps and are another innovative feature inherited from Concept 1. As a result, the rear of the New Beetle looks like its front, in striking contrast to its famous predecessor. Other motorists encountering the car on the road will be in little doubt of the make they are following!

Further echoes are to be found in the aerodynamically honed sills, another Concept 1 inheritance, while the VW monograms in

Top
A New Beetle with chrome-plated customized wheels. This is just the start of a trend

Left and far right
The distinctive VW badges are a notable part of the New Beetle's exterior, However, Mays, who directed the design, insisted that, even if they were removed, there should be no doubt that the car was a Volkswagen. He unquestionably achieved this objective

Right
The fuel filler cap, which is opened from the driver's door

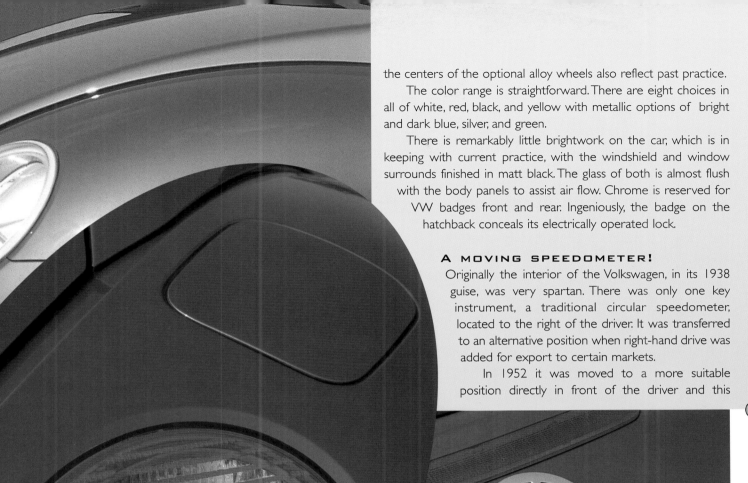

the centers of the optional alloy wheels also reflect past practice.

The color range is straightforward. There are eight choices in all of white, red, black, and yellow with metallic options of bright and dark blue, silver, and green.

There is remarkably little brightwork on the car, which is in keeping with current practice, with the windshield and window surrounds finished in matt black. The glass of both is almost flush with the body panels to assist air flow. Chrome is reserved for VW badges front and rear. Ingeniously, the badge on the hatchback conceals its electrically operated lock.

A MOVING SPEEDOMETER!

Originally the interior of the Volkswagen, in its 1938 guise, was very spartan. There was only one key instrument, a traditional circular speedometer, located to the right of the driver. It was transferred to an alternative position when right-hand drive was added for export to certain markets.

In 1952 it was moved to a more suitable position directly in front of the driver and this

STYLING, INSIDE AND OUT

Below

The VW badge is repeated in the wheel centers and each wheel is equipped with an anti-theft lock. The disc brake caliper can be seen through the wheel spokes

Right

The body-colored door handles echo the Beetle, although they hinge at their rear ends, unlike the 1960s originals

location is reflected in the New Beetle. But a fuel gauge did not arrive on the original until 1962! On the new model this is contained within the speedometer, and its red needle keeps company with a miniature rev counter—something the original car never possessed!

Once seated in the New Beetle the driver cannot ignore this substantial dial that reads— perhaps optimistically—up to 140mph. It also contains a liquid crystal odometer and trip recorder. In addition to the supplementary dials, there are warning lights for the brakes, headlamps and battery. Its blue-hued back lighting is one of the features initiated from the Concept 1 that, happily, has been preserved, and the radio benefits similarly. The Concept 1 also bequeathed this azure tinted light to the instrumentation of the New Beetle's Mark IV Golf first cousin, and it looks like becoming a VW hallmark.

The big circular speedo can be easily viewed through the three-spoke aluminum steering wheel, which can be adjusted for reach as well as rake. It can also be leather-trimmed, but this enhancement only comes with the optional leather seats, of which more later.

The center console contains the eyeball outlets for the air conditioning, which is a standard fitment. Both the ventilation and the car's heating system come complete with dust and pollen filters.

There's a user friendly stereo radio/cassette that is also standard, and its roof-mounted inclined antenna sprouts just above the rear-opening hatch. A CD player is available as an optional extra. Below the stereo are the heating controls and rocker switches for hazard lights and the heated rear window. The console also contains two power output sockets.

The center console contains the air conditioning outlets and the AM/FM radio and cassette player, both of which are standard. In overall appearance, if not detail, it was inherited from Concept 1

Below
The New Beetle can carry four people in comfort and there is a cup holder for everyone. Three are located in front of the gear shift, and there is a single unit concealed in the rear

The big speedometer evokes memories of its predecessor, even if the original never had a rev counter. On the US model, miles per hour dominate, while European and Canadian specification cars feature km/h

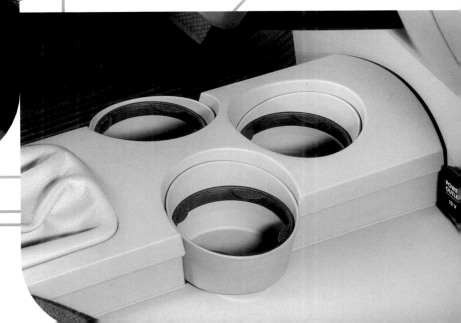

ECHOES OF THE PAST

For the convenience of the driver and front seat passenger, there are cup holders positioned on the transmission tunnel, a provision inherited from the Golf, although there they are provided at facia level.

The passenger also has a dashboard-mounted grab handle, as first offered on the 1954 Beetles. There's another hanging strap on the B-pillar just like the one that arrived with the first of the Export models back in 1949.

Another quirky but somehow perfectly acceptable feature that will strike a familiar note with the older generation is the dashboard-mounted flower vase located to the right of the driver. That must have raised smiles at Wolfsburg when it was first suggested. One of these vases in "cut glass" was available as an option on early 1950s Beetles. And, yes, it was in exactly the same position.

The company likes to identify the new car with the flower power movement of the 1960s when many of its apostles were Beetle drivers. Nowadays, you provide the flower!

The carpeting is also reminiscent of the original, although the Beetle's floor was originally covered with rubber mats until they gave way to a distinctive and particularly durable pile in 1970.

Rear accommodation, as required by the original edict, was always limited, with access being gained by the front seats that tipped forward at their front ends.

It is much the same story with the New Beetle, whose seats are similar to those in the Audi A3 and VW Golf. The fully reclining front seats are of the "easy entry" type, which use Audi's forward folding design for easier access to the rear seats. They automatically spring forward, up and out of the way, when a folding lever is lifted.

Front seat height is variable courtesy of a well proven pump ratchet adjustment system. Heatable front seats are an option, as are heatable windshield washer nozzles.

FINISHING TOUCHES

Upholstery is Primus velour fabric throughout, although there is the option of leatherette and leather on the seating surfaces. Door panels are finished in leatherette, while the upper sill

Above

The passenger's grab handle is yet another reminder of the original Beetle

Above

Like the grab handle, the flower vase is a nostalgic feature that also dates from the 1950s, when the original Beetle was offered with one as an option. It, too, was located to the right of the driver. In addition, it is suggestive of the flower power movement of the following decade and is one of the most talked about New Beetle retro features

Right

The driving compartment, a very pleasing combination of old and new themes. The aluminum spokes of the steering wheel can be adjusted for both height and reach. A bright red is used to illuminate the switches and buttons, while the speedo and radio are lit in green. The anti-theft alarm system, which is standard, protects all the doors, hood, and even the radio

molding is finished in the exterior body color; the exception is the white-painted New Beetle, where these moldings are finished in black.

Despite Volkswagen's claim that the New Beetle is a four seater, in reality it is a two plus two, with plenty of room for two adults in the front and growing children behind—just like the original, in fact.

The similarity ends there, however, because, as the accompanying table reveals, the New Beetle is substantially larger. It has, says Martin Winterkorn, "a unique roomy feeling. For example, the distance between the windshield and dash panel lends a real sense of space to the vehicle."

As befits a modern car, the deeply raked windshield is gently curved. This contrasts with the original, which retained a flat windshield into the 1960s. The 1302 model of 1970, destined for America, featured a mildly convex one and it wasn't until its 1303 derivative appeared in 1972 that a more pronounced element of curvature was, at long last, introduced.

Curves are very much the order of the day on the new car and the driver and passenger benefit from the distinctive roof line. Having said that, its downward sweep, lower than Concept 1's, does reduce rear headroom somewhat.

A power-operated tinted glass sunroof is an option, and is a world away from the old model's cloth sunroof. Windows are manually operated, but electrically activated one-touch up and one-touch down units are available as part of the "Convenience Package," which includes cruise control. The latter is standard on the TDI diesel model.

Below

The detail finishing on the gear shift and handbrake is good. There is additional storage in the front

door nets. Standard trim is Primus velour fabric, although leather and leatherette are available as optional extras

Right

Trunk space is increased when the back seat is folded forward. The spare wheel is underneath

CARRYING CAPACITY

Trunk space is also slightly limited, with a capacity of just 12cu. ft. (0.34sq.m.). However, this is compensated for by good access, with a large hatch and low sill. Carrying capacity can be much improved by folding down the back of the one-piece rear seat.

Once again there is a historical precedent. In the original Beetle, from 1964, the back squab could be folded forward to increase the amount of space available in the car's secondary storage area, located in the deep well behind the seat back.

THE ORIGINAL & NEW BEETLES COMPARED

Beetle 1200		New Beetle
160in (4064mm)	**Length**	161.1in (4092mm)
60in (1524mm)	**Width**	67.9in (1725mm)
57in (1448mm)	**Height**	59.5in (1511mm)
94in (2388mm)	**Wheelbase**	98.9in (2512mm)
5in (1295mm)	**Track-front**	59.6in (1514mm)
49in (1245mm)	**Track-rear**	58.7in (1491mm)
1568lb (711kg)	**Weight**	2717lb (1232kg)

LISTENING TO THE VIEWS OF THE SAFETY LOBBY

One of the factors in the American decline of the original Beetle's popularity was the growth, from the mid-1960s onward, of an increasingly vocal safety lobby. This was coupled with criticisms of the car's handling occasioned by its rear-mounted engine and a perceived lack of frontal collision protection for the occupants. The Golf-based front-wheel-drive New Beetle faces no such limitations and Volkswagen has put great stress on the car's safety features.

In the event of an accident, its occupants will benefit from the protection of an advanced system that comprises a host of state-of-the-art features and structural elements.

At the heart of the passive safety system is the rigid body structure, which incorporates energy-absorbing crumple zones. In the event of a crash these sacrifice themselves in an accordionlike fashion, absorbing energy and thus helping to protect the all important central safety cell that contains the car's occupants. This works in conjunction with a supplementary restraint system.

In addition to the front driver and passenger airbags, the New Beetle uses an innovative seat belt tensioning system that tightens and optimally positions the front belt within milliseconds of a serious impact. These three-point safety belts are also equipped with shoulder height adjustments.

This is one of the first Volkswagens to be fitted with side airbags for the front passengers. No matter how the front occupants adjust their seats, the airbags maintain this protective function. Side protection is further enhanced by structural reinforcement and side members, including anti-intrusion tubes and foam padding in the doors.

Finally there is the obligatory collapsible steering column and steering wheel, which is specially cushioned and designed to manage impact energy.

Such is the New Beetle's comprehensive specification, both inside and out, created for the 21st century but with one eye very much on the past. However, when we come to consider the car's mechanicals in the next chapter, no such nostalgic considerations will be apparent.

> **THERE IS REMARKABLY LITTLE BRIGHTWORK ON THE CAR, WHICH IS IN KEEPING WITH STANDARD PRACTICE...CHROME IS RESERVED FOR VW BADGES FRONT AND REAR**

CHAPTER

3 JOINING THE GOLF CLUB

" OUR BIGGEST HURDLE WAS TRANSPLANTING THAT CUTE COMPACT SHAPE ONTO THE RELATIVELY LARGE GOLF PLATFORM. " HARTMUT WARKUSS, HEAD OF DESIGN, VOLKSWAGEN AG

IT IS WHOLLY appropriate that the New Beetle, as Volkswagen's most important car of recent years, is a synthesis of both the Beetle and the Golf models, the twin pillars of VW's corporate edifice.

As was made clear in the last chapter, while the Beetle has bequeathed the new car the essentials of its distinctive profile, the mechanical components benefit from 24 years of the company's front-wheel-drive expertise, as exemplified in the fourth generation Golf.

Not only is the New Beetle intended to reduce Volkswagen's overdependence on the Golf, it is also a beneficiary of Ferdinand Piëch's ruthless drive on cost cutting. In terms of output, VW is currently Europe's largest car company, and fourth in the world behind General Motors, Ford, and Toyota. Little wonder that chairman Piëch has striven to rationalize components within the group's disparate Audi, Seat, and Skoda makes.

Having said that, because the New Beetle is an unplanned latecomer in the VW model line, an automotive cuckoo in an

DEVELOPMENTS AT VW

otherwise well-ordered corporate nest, some rationalization has had to be sacrificed. But the car will undoubtedly reap dividends for the company wherever its spiritual predecessor was sold—and that's about every country throughout the world.

Paradoxically it was the very success of the Beetle that, by the 1960s, had created a very complacent attitude at Wolfsburg. Deeply rooted in the model's rear mounted, air cooled, horizontally opposed engine, which Europeans call the boxer motor, was an insularity that came close to bringing Germany's largest car company to the brink of financial ruin.

THE COMPANY GROWS

Ironically VW's mechanical salvation, of which the New Beetle is the latest beneficiary, lay in the firm that it bought

Below
Hartmut Warkuss, who saw the New Beetle into production

Above
The modified Golf Mk IV platform that forms the basis of the New Beetle, seen here at the model's sole assembly plant in Puebla, Mexico

Right
The front wheel drive Golf Mark IV which provides the New Beetle with its mechanical components

VW NAMES

The Golf name, incidentally, is not related to the game but refers to the warming waters of the Atlantic's Gulf stream—*Golfstrom* in German. It was one of a trio of climatically related model names then being used by Volkswagen; Passat and Scirocco came courtesy of welcoming trade and hot winds respectively.

from Daimler-Benz in 1965. The Auto Union business dated from the Depression year of 1932 when the Audi, DKW, Horch, and Wanderer companies combined, and this ancestry is reflected in Audi's badge of four linked circles.

Since the war, and with three of the businesses confined behind the Iron Curtain, Auto Union had produced two-stroke, front-wheel-drive cars under the DKW name.

New ownership saw the Audi marque reborn and the company, chaired by Rudolf Leiding, began the production of a new generation of conventional front-wheel-drive, four-stroke models. The most significant of these was the Audi 80 of 1972, a crisply styled sedan powered by a new 1.5 liter, single overhead camshaft, four cylinder engine. It was a worthy recipient of the Car of the Year accolade.

Volkswagen had, in 1970, introduced its own front-wheel-drive model, the K70, another flop, a design that came courtesy

> ❝ MECHANICAL COMPONENTS BENEFIT FROM 24 YEARS OF THE COMPANY'S FRONT WHEEL DRIVE EXPERTISE ❞

of the NSU company it had bought in 1969. Not only was it the first VW to be driven by its front wheels, it was also the first to have a water cooled engine.

But the company was fighting back. Rudolf Leiding had taken over at Wolfsburg in 1971, so he had few inhibitions about drawing on the Ingolstadt company's front-wheel-drive expertise.

THE ARRIVAL OF THE PASSAT, SCIROCCO, AND GOLF

In 1973 VW introduced the Audi 80-related medium size Passat, restyled by Turin-based Ital Design.

March 1974 saw the arrival of the Scirocco hatchback sports coupé, also styled by Ital Design but based on an as yet unseen model that they were also working on.

Thus in June came a light, robust hatchback, which VW had internally coded as EA 337 and which the world now knows as the

Golf. It was the car for which Volkswagen had been waiting. The Golf's design could not have been in greater contrast to the Beetle's and although VW went to great lengths to assure the public that it was not its replacement, there would soon be little point in disguising the fact that it was. Currently, over 17.6 million Golfs have been manufactured by Volkswagen worldwide—that's "only" 4.4 million behind the Beetle.

THE GOLF ENGINE

The fresh air of reality that blew through the corridors of Wolfsburg ensured that the Golf was a front-wheel-drive car. Its water cooled engine was transversely mounted in the manner of the British Mini, and the only specification it had in common with the Beetle was its 94.5in (2400mm) wheelbase. It was to have been powered by a 1.5 liter Wolfsburg-designed unit. Instead, a financially squeezed Volkswagen decided to adopt Audi's existing 1.5 liter four cylinder unit that had begun life, but in an in-line location, in the front wheel drive 80. However, VW developed its own 1.1 liter version.

Both used an iron block and aluminum cylinder head incorporating a single overhead camshaft, actuating two valves per cylinder, and driven by a durable and efficient toothed neoprene belt.

Suspension also differed radically from Wolfsburg's enduring commitment to the Beetle's Porsche-designed torsion bars. At the front the Golf used cheap but effective Ford-pioneered MacPherson struts, which employ coil springs as their suspension medium. At the rear was an innovative coil sprung torsion beam axle, and it says much for the soundness of this combination that the layout, in greatly refined form, is maintained in the current Golf and, in consequence, the New Beetle.

There could soon be little doubt of the Golf's success. As it moved center stage, Beetle production slumped to a little over 450,000 in 1974, and although in that year Wolfsburg stopped building the car, output continued at Volkswagen's Emden factory until it too eventually ceased in 1978.

But the Golf was not just another utilitarian Beetle. It spawned an entire family of cars that went far beyond the original two-model line and transformed VW's hitherto rather staid,

1 The radiator is cooled by twin electric fans, one operating via the air conditioning condensor

2 This car is fitted with the optional 1.9 liter turbocharged diesel engine and, like its gas equivalent, is a four cylinder single overhead camshaft unit

WG
NR 120

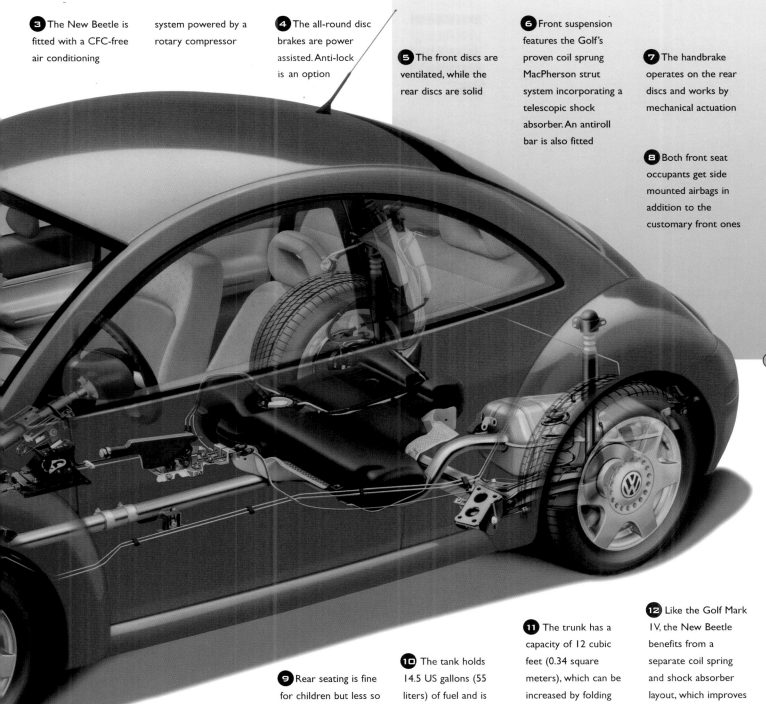

3 The New Beetle is fitted with a CFC-free air conditioning system powered by a rotary compressor

4 The all-round disc brakes are power assisted. Anti-lock is an option

5 The front discs are ventilated, while the rear discs are solid

6 Front suspension features the Golf's proven coil sprung MacPherson strut system incorporating a telescopic shock absorber. An antiroll bar is also fitted

7 The handbrake operates on the rear discs and works by mechanical actuation

8 Both front seat occupants get side mounted airbags in addition to the customary front ones

9 Rear seating is fine for children but less so for adults

10 The tank holds 14.5 US gallons (55 liters) of fuel and is located beneath the rear seat

11 The trunk has a capacity of 12 cubic feet (0.34 square meters), which can be increased by folding the rear seat squab forward

12 Like the Golf Mark IV, the New Beetle benefits from a separate coil spring and shock absorber layout, which improves trunk space

unadventurous image. The New Beetle is a beneficiary of this formidable diversification.

1975—THE GTI

The first of these initiatives, the Golf GTI, arrived in 1975. Credited with beginning the trend for so-called "hot hatchbacks," unusually this project had started life as a private venture by VW engineers. The Golf's light but strong body shell proved an ideal basis for a potent variant. The "I" stood for the Bosch fuel injection system and the 1588cc engine gave the car a top speed of 110mph (177kph), some 15mph (24kph) faster than the 75bhp 1471cc Golf GLS.

With roadholding and acceleration to match, the GTI would account for an impressive 10 percent of Golf sales and it remains an integral part of the model line to this day.

The imminent demise of the German-built Beetle meant that Volkswagen would have been left without an open-top car, so in 1979 the company announced the introduction of the Golf cabriolet produced, like its famous forebear, by Karmann of Osnabruck.

In 1982 came an economy conscious diesel version of the Golf. Available in 1.5 and 1.6 liter forms, it also broke new ground

Above

This is the optional 1.9 liter turbocharged diesel TDI engine—although it's difficult to see the unit beneath its strong protective plastic cover. Unlike the Golf Mk III GTI

unit opposite, it is shared with the latest Golf and drives the front wheels via a manual or automatic gearbox

Right

The 2.0 liter gas fueled four cylinder is the standard engine and, apart from a new aluminum crossflow cylinder head, is inherited from the Golf Mark III

ENGINE OPTIONS

FOR THE FUTURE

The engines shown here are to be joined in 1998 by a further

option in the shape of the 1.8 liter 150bhp turbocharged unit, as

fitted to the Golf GTI

because it was the first power unit of its type in the world to be based on the block of the gasoline engine (because of the high compression ratios involved, diesels had hitherto employed far more robust castings.).

The resulting light, high revving four had the customers queuing up and the diesel soon accounted for a massive 25 percent of Golfs sold in Germany; by 1982 this figure had doubled. Little wonder that VW emerged as the world's largest manufacturer of diesel engines.

THE ORIGINS OF THE NEW BEETLE'S TURBO DIESEL ENGINE

In that same year of 1982 this concept was taken one stage further with the arrival of the 1.6 liter Golf turbo diesel. This offered the traditional economy associated with a compression ignition engine but the exhaust-driven turbocharger endowed it with the acceleration of a gasoline unit. It could thus reach 60mph (97kph) in around 13 seconds and had a claimed top speed of 96mph (155kph). The turbo diesel has been a popular Golf option ever since and, once again, the New Beetle is an inheritor of

Right

The engine/transmission unit on the assembly line. The ventilated front disc brakes are clearly visible

this long established variant.

In 1977, two years after the introduction of the Golf and with its popularity assured, Volkswagen began to plan its successor. But should it develop a wholly different vehicle or opt, instead, for the evolutionary approach of a more refined car which outwardly and mechanically resembled its predecessor? The success of Nordhoff's strategy with the Beetle provided a formidable and inescapable precedent and Wolfsburg opted for it again.

So, when the second version of the corporately styled Golf arrived in 1983, after approximately six million examples of the initial range had been built the world over, it was larger, faster and quieter than the Mark I. However, in virtually every area the new

Golf was clearly related to the old.

It was a similar story the second time around, although this series was destined to be even more popular than the first, It similarly lasted for eight years, and by the time output ceased in 1991 no less than 6.7 million had been manufactured.

The variations that arrived with the first generation Golfs were perpetuated and in 1988 came yet another in the form of a fashionable four-wheel-drive system. Called the Syncro, it gave its name to an enhanced low volume version of the Golf.

The third generation of the family arrived in 1991. As the model had evolved, so the capacities of its engines increased, although their overall design remained essentially unchanged.

Enlargement came mostly through the adoption of longer strokes, with the intention of improving torque, refinement, fuel consumption, and noise levels. The Golf GTI version was powered by an enlarged 1984cc unit, which survived until the model's replacement by the fourth generation cars in 1997. It is this overhead camshaft four that forms the basis of the gasoline engine that is the standard fitment in the New Beetle.

Its original optional unit also dates, in essence, from the 1991 Golf and is the turbocharged direct injection diesel TDI version that appeared in 1896cc form and was also used in the Audi 80, A3, and A4 cars. (Since 1994 Audi has adopted a simple A-prefix for its model names.)

It was during the production of this third Golf that the Volkswagen corporation underwent a series of structural and management changes, the effects of which are still being felt.

VW BUY SKODA AND SEAT

In 1982 Carl Hahn, who had successfully run Volkswagen of America during the growth years of 1959–64, became VW's chairman, and he initiated an era of corporate expansion. The collapse of communism in Europe in 1989 allowed VW to buy the Trabant factory in the former East Germany, for burgeoning Golf production. More significantly, in 1991 it took control of the

Czechoslovakian Skoda business. This followed the purchase of Seat, Fiat's former Spanish subsidiary, in 1986.

Volkswagen thus became a four marque company, but this growth produced its own problems for a combine that was still operated, in some respects, as diverse unrationalized entities. Although four cylinder engines were by then freely exchanged between Volkswagen and Audi, in 1991 each firm extravagantly introduced its own but wholly different V6 power unit of the same 2.8 liter capacity.

FERDINAND PIËCH RATIONALIZES

Once again it was the Ingolstadt company which provided Volkswagen with its next chairman. Following Hahn's retirement, Ferdinand Piëch arrived at Wolfsburg at the beginning of 1993 and pledged to cut costs and radically revitalize the VW management. Within three years there were no remaining members—with one exception—of the 10-strong board of management he had inherited. And the sole survivor—research and development mandarin Ulrich Seiffert—has the dubious distinction of having been fired twice!

The principal problem that faced Piëch was how to limit the number of costly platforms used within the newly extended Volkswagen group. A policy was initiated that reduced an already rationalized sixteen to just four. When completed, VW estimated it would produce annual savings of some DM3 billion.

THE A-CLASS PLATFORM

The New Beetle is based on the corporate A-class platform and work on it began early in 1993. The intention was that, worldwide, a single set of tools would be used for every car incorporating the unit. Until the appearance of the revived Beetle, this rigorous policy was strictly adhered to and Horst König, who is in charge of the program, revealed in 1997 that "we need board approval for any change: even drilling a hole is not possible without the board's OK."

The platform possesses what the industry describes as 20 "hard points" to which essential components are attached. But, as will emerge, the New Beetle did not conform to this seemingly inviolate strategy.

The platform made its first public debut, in albeit truncated form, at the 1995 Frankfurt Motor Show on the Audi TT coupé concept car. This Audi was also the work of the versatile Mays and was conceived, like the New Beetle, at the corporate Simi Valley Design Center, and was similarly destined for the production line.

PLATFORM

A platform is a car's floorpan to which common running gear, in other words the suspension and steering components, are attached.

What VW has invariably done is to add an engine to a platform, while the persona of the Volkswagen, Audi, Skoda, and Seat makes is maintained by the adoption of a variety of body styles and by tuning a standard suspension in different ways.

At the end of 1995 the platform again went public, at the Tokyo Motor Show, this time on the Wolfsburg-refined version of Concept 1. However, the following June the platform did finally go into volume production—on the three door Audi A3 hatchback. It was effectively a more expensive and sporty version of the yet unseen fourth generation Golf.

A consequence of using the new platform was that, for the first time, Audi bowed to the Golf's transversely located engine; hitherto its front wheel drive cars had featured distinctive in-line power units.

The next model to have the A-platform as its basis was the Skoda Octavia five door hatchback that appeared three months after the Audi, in September 1996. However, its principal application was the new Golf, announced in August 1997. The third generation Golf had accounted for sales of 4.9 million, which was less than the previous two, but then it had only had a production span of six years, as opposed to eight.

THE GOLF

The new Golf similarly resembled its predecessor but VW have deliberately introduced curved windshield pillars and pronounced wheel arches to articulate its new house style, most clearly exemplified by the New Beetle.

It was offered with a total of eight engines, ranging in capacity from 1.4 to 1.9 liters. These included the 90bhp TDI turbocharged diesel used in the New Beetle which was also available in the new Golf TDI. The more powerful of two GTI variants uses Audi's proven 20 valve 1.8 liter turbo gasoline fuelled four. This 150bhp unit, inherited from the VW Passat, will be available in a sports version of the New Beetle for the 1999 model year. For now, the gasoline engine in the New Beetle is the eight valve 115bhp 2.0 liter unit from the Golf GTI Mk III.

Announced in January 1998, the car that is the subject of this book was the fourth recipient of VW's A-platform and the fifth and sixth cars followed in Fall 1998. The same platform also provides the basis of the S5 replacement for the five door Seat Toledo hatchback and the New Beetle's Audi TT first cousin.

The latest manifestation of the Beetle differed structurally from its five stablemates because of its unconventional body style. Another unusual feature of its development was that the VW group's production models do not usually begin life as concept cars—with the exception of the Audi TT.

MODIFYING THE PLATFORM

But most significantly, the radical nature of its idiosyncratic and curvilinear Beetle-related bodywork meant that the hitherto inviolate

Left
Before being united with its platform, the New Beetle's body passes through a 26-step anticorrosion process. On a good day some 400 will leave Volkswagen's factory at Puebla, Mexico, which produces a total of 1500 cars daily. The original Beetle is still built at the same site, although assembly methods are rather more basic

Right
The baking process.
The New Beetle's
body is fully
galvanized. It is
reminiscent of the
original Beetle, which
had an excellent

reputation for the
quality of its
paintwork. One of its
most famous
advertisements stated:
"After we paint the
car we paint the paint"

sanctity of the platform parameters had to be sacrificed. As the comment at the beginning of this chapter by VW's design chief, Harmut Warkuss, makes clear, this was the most demanding aspect of the New Beetle's design process.

This departure from the corporate norm was also mentioned by Martin Winterkorn, head of Volkswagen's technical development, at the model's 1998 press launch. "We are using the proven Volkswagen platform strategy; this gave us the opportunity to create an outstanding automobile economically," he told his audience. "Still, *more than fifty percent of the platform* [author's italics] had to be modified in order to adjust the unique New Beetle body to fit."

Happily the suspension required little modification and is therefore closely related to Volkswagen's other A-cars. But it takes into account that the New Beetle turns the scales at 2712lb (1230kg), 52lb (23.5kg) heavier than the Golf's 2660lb (1207kg).

> **❝ THE LATEST BEETLE DIFFERED STRUCTURALLY FROM ITS STABLEMATES BECAUSE OF ITS UNCONVENTIONAL BODY STYLE ❞**

SUSPENSION

At the front the MacPherson strut with control arms and antiroll or sway bar layout has been tailored for power-assisted steering, which is fitted as standard across the Mark IV Golf range. This enhanced rack and pinion system is thus inherited by the New Beetle. Similarly, at the rear is a refined version of the V-profiled independent torsion beam axle featured on the Mark III Golf that reaches back to the model's 1974 origins. But for the fourth generation car, and thus the New Beetle, the damper and coil springs have been separated. The advantage of this divergence of components is that the latter can be positioned under the side members, which allows more room in the car's luggage compartment at the rear.

Further space saving in that area is achieved by the use of gas filled dampers, because the suspension turrets no longer intrude into the trunk area.

BRAKES AND WHEELS

Brakes are allround discs, and the 10.6in (269mm) diameter components are front ventilated. They had hitherto only featured at the top of the Mark III Golf range and its successor is similarly uprated, although it uses larger diameter 14in (356mm) units.

Anti-lock brakes are specified on the Golf although they are an optional feature on the New Beetle.

The New Beetle has large 6.5Jx16in black finished steel wheels fitted as standard. However, they are smaller than those used on Concept 1, which used 18in wheels. The 16in diameter is more appropriate because it corresponds to that of the original Beetle, although they are about twice the width, to the benefit of the New Beetle's stability and ride.

Six spoke alloy wheels are available as an option. These are of essentially the same design as those fitted to Concept 1 and are of the same reduced dimensions as the steel ones. The VW logo hub caps are a clear echo of past practice, and the wheels are fitted with antitheft locks.

Engine

On its announcement the car was offered with a choice of two transversely located engines. Standard fitment is the gasoline fueled 2 liter, four cylinder, cast iron, eight valve unit with a robust five bearing crankshaft. This is the engine that powered the Mark III Golf GTI.

It has been significantly updated, with a new aluminum cylinder head of the efficient crossflow variety. The belt driven, single overhead camshaft that actuates two valves per cylinder, via maintenance free hydraulic tappets, follows established Golf practice. Fully mapped electronic ignition is employed with a distributorless coil block. Cooling is by a front mounted radiator and a thermostatically controlled two-speed electric fan.

The 82.5x92.8mm, 1984cc unit develops 115bhp at 5400rpm. Sequential multiport Motronic fuel injection is fitted, while the emissions system is a three-way catalytic converter with two oxygen sensors, and a fuel evaporation system.

Right
The spraying process continues with computer controlled nozzles ensuring an even distribution. Laser welding guarantees consistent build quality and closely fitting body panels

abrupt diesel cut out. It is naturally more economical than the gasoline engine, with stated EPA figures of 41 and 48mpg for city and highway driving on the manual gearbox, giving a range of close on 700 miles (1126km) from a 14.5 US gallon (55 liter) fuel tank. Figures of 34 and 44 mpg respectively are recorded for the automatic version.

Although these two engines were available at the car's launch, a third power unit was introduced later in the year. This is the 1.8 liter, twin overhead camshaft, turbocharged Audi engine, with five valves per cylinder, that was offered on the Mark IV version of the Golf GTI. Developing 150bhp at 5700rpm, it endowed that car with refined performance and a 139mph (224kph) top speed, and should also work wonders for the—albeit heavier—New Beetle to provide a desirable, although not quite as rapid, version.

The American version of the New Beetle is tailored to the country's increasingly stringent emissions regulations in accordance with a 50 state certification for gasoline and diesel engines. As a TLEV—transitional low emission vehicle—it is also suitable for use in the environmentally conscious state of California, as well as in Massachusetts and New York City.

FUEL CONSUMPTION

Volkswagen statistics give a city consumption EPA (Environmental Protection Agency) figure of 27mpg and 29mpg on the highway with this engine, when used in conjunction with the standard five-speed manual gearbox. The respective figures are 22 and 27 mpg when the optional four-speed electronically controlled automatic transmission is fitted. It uses adaptive learning to personalize shift patterns according to an individual's driving styles.

More economical is the optional 1.9 liter TDI diesel four, which combines respectable performance with good fuel economy. In well established Volkswagen tradition it shares many features with the gasoline fueled four. A feature of this type of diesel unit is that fuel is injected directly and ignited in the cylinder head, thanks to an advanced electronic control unit.

The 79.5 × 95.5mm (1896cc) four has developed an excellent reputation for its good low speed flexibility. Refinement is an ongoing process for Volkswagen and the Golf IV—and thus the New Beetle—and the TDI benefits from the introduction of an electronically controlled shutoff flap in the inlet manifold. This allows the engine to come to a gentle stop when the ignition is switched off, rather than the hitherto characteristic

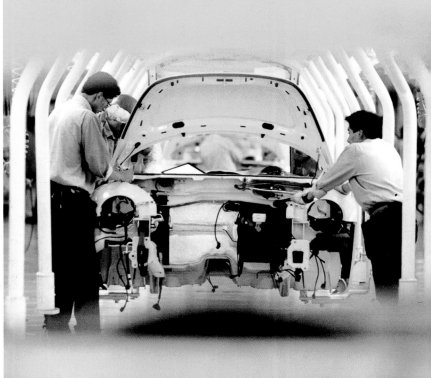

CHAPTER

4 LAUNCH AND RECEPTION

"BY DINT OF ... ITS AVANT-GARDE INTERIOR, AND ITS COQUETTISH EXTERIOR STYLING, IT REGISTERS AN EASY EIGHT ON THE C/D GRIN METER. " CAR & DRIVER, FEB 1998

THE NORTH AMERICAN International Auto Show, held at Detroit's Cobo Center, opened its doors to the public on January 10th, 1998. It was unprecedented for a new Volkswagen to be launched outside Germany, yet such was the importance the company attached to the New Beetle's potential American sales that it was unveiled there, in the motor city of Detroit, four years after Concept 1 had taken the event by storm.

VW's confidence appears to have been well placed, judging by

THE CAR IS LAUNCHED

the sensational reception the model has been accorded in the US that shows little sign of abating. The response has even taken Volkswagen aback and it has upped its first year sales target from an initial 50,000 to 65,000 cars. The omens look good.

However, the press had an opportunity to acquaint itself with the car five days before, on January 5th. There, in 18,000 square feet (1672 square meters) of floor space at the Center, Volkswagen of America had created a room within a room for what it described as the model's world premiere. And despite the fact that the car's appearance was well known, the corporate show stand was concealed behind white curtains.

The press conference, which opened at 9.15 a.m., was chaired by Clive Warrilow, president and chief executive of Volkswagen of America. He set the pace for the proceedings when he declared: "Some may have predicted a retro car but ... the New Beetle is a completely modern design, almost futuristic. It is designed to appeal to people who fondly recall the past, as well as young people who have no connection at all to the original.

"Where the original Beetle provided basic transportation, the New Beetle is an upmarket, lifestyle vehicle. It's highly emotional, a car that makes the experience of driving fun again."

The significance of the launch was reflected by the fact that it was attended by the usually Wolfsburg-domiciled key players in the car's creation and evolution. Company chairman Ferdinand Piëch was there, along with Martin Winterkorn, in charge of technical development, and Jens Neumann, who, like Piëch, hailed from VW's Audi subsidiary and is Volkswagen's finance director.

The chairman declared: "We believe that the New Beetle is not just another car. It will stand out on North American roads." With a clear reference to the complacency that the original Beetle had wrought in Volkswagen's ranks in the 1960s, Dr. Piëch pledged, "Despite all the high expectations we have for the New Beetle, one thing is also for sure: Volkswagen will never be again the one-car 'Beetle-company.'"

WORLD REACTION

Dr. Neumann provided some of the background of how the public responded to the model's gestation. During the four years since

Concept 1's arrival "we have received thousands of letters and phone calls from around the world. People offering ideas, sharing personal stories and asking us again and again: 'Are you really bringing the Beetle back?' "

"The answer is, 'No, we are not bringing the Beetle back. We bring you the New Beetle.' "

He revealed that the car would be on sale in the US, Canada, and Mexico by the end of March; European exports would begin in the fall, while the rest of the world would have to wait until 1999.

"The New Beetle will reinforce the emotional link to our customers and friends. The emotion will appeal to both men and women, both young and young-at-heart. This is the car for people who see the world's glass as half full . . . it's original, honest and timeless, and it truly represents the core values of Volkswagen."

The company believed that as these values appeal to an audience that transcends class and social status, it would expect to take "New Beetle lovers" from a wide variety of competitors and market segments.

"You might wonder how we plan to market this car to such a broad audience." Dr. Neumann then revealed what is probably a unique public response to a motor vehicle that goes beyond the customary corporate hype often pervading such occasions.

"Wherever and whenever we showed the New Beetle design concepts, we noticed an amazing reaction. People of all nationalities, of all ages, divergent life experiences, different incomes, different religions—all behaved the same way when they first saw the car. They smiled."

Following its unveiling, reaction to the car was overwhelmingly favorable. Tom Janiszewski, who was reporting for the British magazine, *VW Motoring*, found that "the overall mood about the car was very positive. The media on hand at the unveiling seemed very impressed. This was confirmed when their TV and newspaper reports were released literally hours after the unveiling.

"The New Beetle was immediately named the star of the show." This honor had previously been bestowed on such local products as Chrysler's

Above left and below
The New Beetle's stylish ring-bound instruction book

Above
The model on display in a US showroom. They don't remain on

sale there for long, as demand is high, VW having already increased initial sales estimates

Plymouth Prowler or Dodge Viper.

Janiszewski found that, after the show had closed, "the New Beetle has gained the interest of the general American public. Many VW dealers already have customers on waiting lists for the car . . ."

Seven weeks later, at the end of February, Ferdinand Piëch hosted a second launch, this time for 300 representatives of the world's motoring press, who gathered expectantly at the Atlanta Horse Park, Georgia.

Unlike the Detroit premiere, there was an opportunity to drive some of the 55 New Beetles brought in for the occasion. At the presentation, Piëch candidly revealed that, initially, Volkswagen's Wolfsburg-based engineers had been reluctant to work on the New Beetle. This was because it reminded them of how close the company had come to disaster when it had not replaced the original soon enough.

But they gradually responded to the model and became enthusiastic. Piëch conceded: "We may have underestimated the emotion and desire for the car."

As the grandson of Ferdinand Porsche, who designed the original Beetle, the usually unemotional Piëch was clearly moved by the audience's response to his words.

DIFFERENT OPTIONS

The car went on sale in the following month, March, and in America the entry level version, with a gas fueled 2 liter engine and manual five speed transmission, sold for a lower than anticipated $15,200. The diesel powered 1.9 TDI cost an extra $1275 and thus had a selling price of $16,475.

While orders could be taken for these basic models, for the first few months of

manufacture all cars were produced with a so-called Sport Package that cost an extra $410. This is what VW designates its P4 option, and provides the new owner with alloy wheels and projector beam halogen fog lamps.

Across the border, in Canada, the same Sport equipment applies but the prices there for the gas and diesel fueled versions are $19,940 and $21,685 respectively.

Let's take a closer look at the various options available. There are five in all and the P1 designation is accorded to what VW calls its Convenience Package. This offers a cruise control, which is standard on the TDI, and electrically powered windows.

The Partial Leather Interior carries the P2 name. As already noted, the leather finish is applied not just to the seating surfaces and steering wheel, but also to the shift knob, its boot and the handbrake cover. By contrast, P3 has leatherette trim with perforated seat panels.

The P4 Sport Pack has already been mentioned while the last of the options, the P5, is the Cold Weather Package, which gives heated front seats and windshield washer nozzles.

All models can be fitted with an electrically operated sunroof and anti-lock brakes. Customers who require the CD player, ashtray, and cigarette lighter can apply to their local dealers to have them fitted.

These are all, of course, left-hand-drive cars; their right-hand-drive equivalents are not planned to appear before mid-1999, when Britain and Japan should get their first supplies. And if the razzmatazz that greeted the New Beetle in America is any precedent, demand should be considerable.

THE MEXICAN TRADITION

As already mentioned, the original Beetle is still being built at Volkswagen's Mexican factory at Puebla, some 90 miles northwest of Mexico City. About 50,000 will be produced in 1998 and one of these will be the 22 millionth Beetle. A total of 1.5 million have been made in Mexico since 1965.

But, more significantly, this is the sole New Beetle assembly plant, as the economic arguments for building the car there are compelling. Not only is Mexico adjacent to what is, arguably, the model's largest potential market, but above all wages are considerably less than in Europe and America.

A total of 8200 employees are each paid $8 a day ($15 if benefits are included). And if that doesn't sound very much, it is five times Mexico's national minimum wage. They each work a seven hour daily shift six days a week, and it is this key ingredient which allows Volkswagen to market the New Beetle at a highly competitive price.

On an assembly line essentially the same as the Mark IV Golf facility in Wolfsburg, Puebla produces some 400 New Beetles a day, around a quarter of the factory's total, when output reaches the customary 1500 mark. It also builds the third generation Golf and Golf Cabriolet for the American market as well as the Vento, the sedan version of the Golf, sold under the old Jetta name in the US. Puebla's 1997 output was 265,000 cars, but, with the New Beetle coming on stream, the 1998 figure could be as high as 450,000.

With North America as the New Beetle's sole export market at first, any design or manufacturing problems that show themselves are going to be relatively close to home.

Two months after its launch, in May, Volkswagen of America announced that it was recalling some 8500 cars sold in the US and about 1600 examples bought by Canadians. An underhood chafing problem with the car's electrical wiring had been identified that could have resulted in the air conditioning compressor malfunctioning.

Such glitches are not uncommon on a newly introduced model and this one has done nothing to dent the extraordinary reception that has greeted the New Beetle in the US.

AMERICAN REACTIONS

Automobile magazine experienced the phenomenon at first hand when it decided to drive a red 2 liter New Beetle the 3800 miles (6100km) across the continent from San Francisco to New York.

Throughout the journey the car generated an unflagging public response and its occupants were invariably asked the same four

Left
A New Beetle enhanced by Neuspeed of Camarillo, California. The 53 number comes courtesy of Herbie, a Beetle that starred in four Hollywood films of the 1968/80 era

Above, center
Herbie's number again, this time on an Audi 1.8 turbo engined New Beetle entered for German races in 1998 by Australian Ross Palmer

Above
New Beetle owner Bobby Price of Fayetteville, New Carolina, has already customized his car with Neeper Intake rims, rear spoiler and

front bug guard, while inside he enjoys the sound of a Kicker audio system

questions, one of which harked back to a memorable failing of the original! People wanted to know if it was the New Beetle, what it cost, whether its heater was any good, and whether the engine was in the rear.

But once on the highway, the magic really began to work. "...People are letting us change lanes...They're smiling, they're waving. They're letting us out of gas stations in front of them. They're giving the thumbs up."

Not only did the public seem to like the car but writer Jean Jennings found "the seat wonderfully supportive," although she did have reservations about some other elements: "The headrests are tortuous for snoozing," she said; using the seemingly distant sun vizor "was like reaching for the moon," and on the trip she only averaged 23.5 miles per gallon.

QUIET PERFORMER

Car and Driver magazine liked the New Beetle too. When pressed, the car felt as composed as a Golf, although there was rather more body roll than expected. "...it's not only affordable but usable 365 days a year. What's more, it made everyone smile. Even Piëch. If there's a serious downside to this car, we haven't yet found it."

Gert Hack tested a California-registered yellow 1.9 liter TDI for Britain's *Autocar* magazine. "Climb into the New Beetle and the immediate impression is one of space." This was on account of the Multi Purpose Vehicle-like dashboard that pushed the windshield forward of the front passengers, the result, in part, of the adoption of the Golf platform.

The downside was that "while the distinctive curved roof line frees up plenty of space in the front seats, it restricts head room badly in the rear."

As far as performance was concerned, it came as little surprise that, at higher speeds, "the Beetle behaves pretty much like the Golf, which means it's a capable and mature-handling car but a little underwhelming in terms of pure driver appeal."

The reception that the New Beetle has been accorded by the American press accurately mirrors the public mood, and even the White House has been in the vanguard of "New Beetle Mania." For when Chelsea Clinton returned to Washington after her first year

at Stanford University in June, she found that her parents had bought her a New Beetle.

She'll be seeing plenty more on the nation's freeways. Within months of the model's arrival in the showrooms, demand was such that potential customers were reported to be traveling to other states to secure a car—and this was regardless of their color requirements and preferred options. The waiting list is now reported to stretch to the year 2000.

People are said to have been following transporters delivering cars to dealers and they have then been prepared to pay over list price. Volkswagen has apparently strictly informed its retail outlets not to sell cars abroad, whatever the incentives. Despite this ruling, some New Beetles have found their way to Europe, and a handful have appeared on British roads.

A BRITISH VIEWPOINT

For much of the 1960s the Beetle was the UK's best-

selling imported car and, in consequence, there are numerous clubs devoted to its running and restoration. But how did those dyed-in-the-wool enthusiasts view the New Beetle when they believe that the only real Volkswagen is one with its air cooled engine firmly planted in the rear?

VW Motoring canvassed their views. Richard Copping of the Historic VW Club spoke for many of his like-minded contemporaries when he said: "I don't really like the shape and styling, for it is almost like a cartoon version of the original Beetle, but one which suffers from the wildest extremes of the designers' desire to be topical and perhaps a touch outlandish."

A contrary view was provided by Volkswagen authority and author Robin Wager, who considered that, in a radically changed world, there was still room for what he dubbed the Classic and New Beetle. "But let's give VW credit for this boldness and, if somebody wants to make their style statement, it's better they should drive to the supermarket in a turbo-diesel New Beetle than a gas-guzzling 4 x 4!"

So much for the cognoscenti, but what of the man and woman in the street? Although the car will not go on sale in the UK until mid-1999, *Autocar*'s Colin Goodwin, who has owned a couple of Beetles himself, drove one around London.

One passerby, Ken Burley, has owned Beetles since the 1960s and, although he initially loved the new car, he thought it would be too small for him. But the more he looked at it, the more he started to talk like an interested buyer rather than just an interested enthusiast.

Another driver was a Mercedes-Benz owner and avowed Beetle-hater. But he also responded positively to the car. Not only did he like the looks but also the interior. Goodwin believes that the New Beetle is set to repeat its American success in England. And his final opinion on the car? "I expected to be lukewarm about the Beetle, but I loved it. It's a fun car, pure and simple."

GERMAN RESPONSES

A trickle of cars is also beginning to appear on the roads of Germany, although at one point early in 1998 Ferdinand Piëch was the only New Beetle driver in the country!

An example of the New Beetle was taken by the magazine *auto motor und sport* onto the streets of Stuttgart to see what the German public thought of the car. It was an appropriate location because it was in that city that Ferdinand Porsche designed the original Volkswagen in the 1930s.

The New Beetle got a very mixed reception. Frank-Albert Illg and Malte Jurgens of the nostalgic *Classic Motorcycle* magazine both responded impassively to the car. The latter, "stony faced," did not react, "not even to the waving marigold" in the bud vase.

The latter feature did, however, produce a positive response from 92 year old Adelbert Schaar, who is the proud owner of a 1967 Beetle. But he couldn't understand "the Beetle mania" although he liked the vase, which must have struck a nostalgic note.

On the autobahn the New Beetle produced similar emotions to those experienced by *Automobile*'s correspondents in the States. Lady drivers who encountered it "burst into laughter and

Top left
Some of the first of many New Beetle models that have been produced for enthusiasts of all ages

Below and left
Over the years there have been many models of the original on sale and the New Beetle looks like being

no exception. This is one of the more sophisticated examples, coming complete with its own radio control unit

But, above all, there can no doubting that the Beetle is its spiritual inspiration, and such has been the success of the car in America that, by the summer of '98, it was reported that Volkswagen was contemplating commissioning one of its European plants to cope with anticipated demand from the Old World. It has yet to confirm this, although it has said that the model can be built anywhere that the Golf is built, and this includes Wolfsburg, home of the original Beetle . . . .

[blew] kisses to the occupants of the Beetle."

Come the new year, there will be plenty more New Beetles in Germany as October sees the model's European debut at the Paris Motor Show.

THE NEW BEETLE EVOLVES

Further variations are inevitable. It must only be a matter of time before a cabriolet version arrives and VW design director Hartmut Warkuss has intimated that the company is contemplating commissioning well known artists to create distinctive color schemes and upholstery materials.

New mechanical options for the future must include the fitment of Volkswagen's compact VR6 engine that is already used in the related Mark IV Golf. As already noted, the 1.8 liter 20 valve twin-cam turbo unit is to be made available. And then there is VW's four wheel drive Syncro system that could also find its way under the model's curvaceous bodywork.

However, there is nothing to stop enthusiasts shoehorning more powerful engines under the New Beetle's hood. Although it has only been on the market for six months, the transplant business has already started.

What is probably the fastest New Beetle on the road resides in Germany and is the work of Roland Mayer's Motoren-Technik-Mayer tuning business. He has beaten Wolfsburg at its own game and replaced the standard engine with the Golf's twin-cam 20 valve turbo unit, tuned to MTM's Stage 2 specifications, with no less than 240bhp on tap.

His corporately decaled white New Beetle, enhanced by a carbon/kevlar front air splitter, lowered suspension, upgraded brakes and five spoke alloy wheels courtesy of a Porsche 911 Carrera 4S, proclaims the presence of a mean-looking and formidable performer. One hundred miles an hour (161kph) comes up in a shade under 17 seconds while top speed is a raucous 148mph (238kph). But it can only be a matter of time before Mayer is overtaken.

So welcome to the world of the New Beetle. With such a pedigree this is a model that will run and run!

ENGINE	gasoline	diesel
Type	Four cylinder, in-line	Four cylinder, in-line
Bore x stroke	82.5 x 92.8mm	79.5 x 95.5mm
Displacement	1984cc (121.1cu. in)	1896cc (115.7cu. in)
Compression ratio	10.0:1	19.5:1
Horsepower (DIN)	115 @ 5200rpm	90 @ 4000rpm
Max. torque, lbs-ft	122 @ 2600rpm	149 @ 1900rpm
Fuel requirement	regular unleaded	diesel

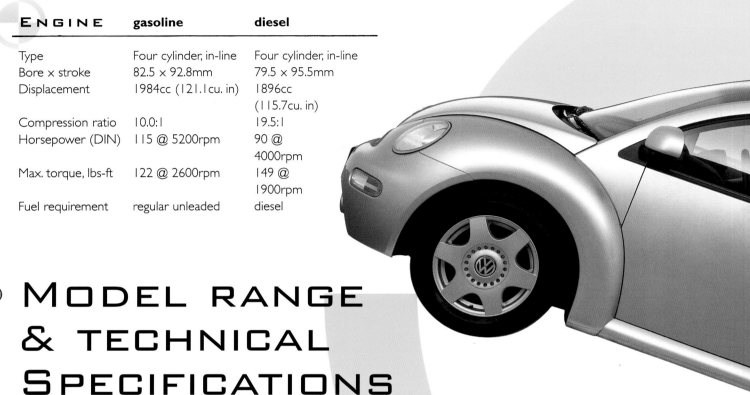

MODEL RANGE & TECHNICAL SPECIFICATIONS

ENGINE DESIGN

Arrangement	front mounted, transverse
Cylinder block	cast iron
Crankshaft	cast iron, five main bearings
Cylinder head	aluminum alloy, crossflow
Valve gear	single overhead camshaft, cogged-tooth belt driven, two valves per cylinder, maintenance free hydraulic lifters
Cooling system	water cooled, water pump, crossflow radiator, thermostatically controlled two speed electric radiator fan
Lubrication	rotary gear pump, chain driven, water cooled oil cooler
Fuel/air supply	sequential multiport fuel injection Bosch Motronic 5.92
Emissions system	OBD 2, three-way catalytic converter with two oxygen sensors (upstream and downstream), enhanced evaporation system, Onboard Refueling Vapor Recovery (ORVR)

CAPACITIES

Engine oil (with filter)	4.8qt	(4.54lit)
Fuel tank	14.5gal	(55lit)
Cooling system	6.7qt	(6.34lit)

ELECTRICAL SYSTEM

Alternator, volts/amps	14/90
Battery, volts (amp hrs)	12 (60)
Ignition	digital electronic, distributorless coil block with knock sensor
Firing order	1-3-4-2

STEERING

Type	rack and pinion, power assisted
Turns (lock to lock)	3.2
Turning circle (curb to curb)	32.8ft (10m)
Ratio	17.8:1

INTERIOR VOLUME—SAE

EPA class	subcompact	EPA
Passenger volume	84.3cu.ft (2.4cu.m)	84 (2.38cu.m)
Truck volume	12.0 (0.34cu.m)	12 (0.34cu.m)
Seating capacity	four	
	front	**rear**
Volume	49.7cu.ft (1.4cu.m)	34.6 (0.98cu.m)
Head room	41.3in (1049mm)	36.7 (932mm)
Shoulder room	52.8in (1341mm)	49.4 (1255mm)
Leg room	39.4in (1000mm)	33.0 (838mm)

FUEL CONSUMPTION

	5-speed manual		4-speed automatic	
	GASOLINE	DIESEL	GASOLINE	DIESEL
City	23mpg	41mpg	22mpg	34mpg
Highway	29mpg	48mpg	27mpg	44mpg

DRIVE TRAIN

Configuration			front-wheel-drive	
Gear ratios	**5-speed manual**		**4-speed automatic**	
	GASOLINE	DIESEL	GASOLINE	DIESEL
1st	3.78:1	3.50:1	2.74:1	2.71:1
2nd	2.12:1	1.94	1.55:1	1.44:1
3rd	1.36:1	1.23:1	1.00:1	1.00:1
4th	1.03:1	0.84:1	0.68:1	0.74:1
5th	0.84:1	0.68:1		
Reverse	3.60:1	3.60:1	2.11:1	2.88:1
Final drive	4.24:1	3.89:1	4.88:1	3.63:1

BODY, CHASSIS, AND SUSPENSION

Type	unitary steel construction, bolt-on fenders, front and rear bumper covers in thermoplastic olefin (TPO)
Front suspension	independent by MacPherson struts, coil springs, telescopic shock absorbers, stabilizer bar
Rear suspension	independent by torsion beam axle, coil springs, telescopic shock absorbers, stabilizer bar
Brake system	power-assisted, dual circuit 10.6in (280mm) vented front discs and 9.0in (239mm) solid rear discs
Anti-lock braking system	optional, Teves, 3 channel ABS
Parking brake	mechanical, on rear wheels
Wheels	61/2 J x 16, steel with full wheel covers, five bolts (alloys optional)
Tires	205/55 R 16H all seasons
Drag coefficient	0.38

DIMENSIONS

Wheelbase	98.9in	(2512mm)		
Track	**front**		**rear**	
	59.6in	(1514mm)	58.7in	(1491mm)
Overall length	161.1in	(4092mm)		
Overall width	67.9in	(1725mm)		
Overall height	59.5in	(1511mm)		
Ground clearance	4.2in	(107mm)		
Curb weight	**5-speed manual**		**4-speed automatic**	
	2712lb	(1230kg)	2778lb	(1260kg)
Payload	992lb	(450kg)	936lb	(425kg)

PRICES

	New Beetle	**New Beetle TDI**
America	$15,200	$16,475
Canada	$19,940	$21,685

EVER SINCE THE 1960S, when America led the way in legislation, safety considerations have played an increasingly important part in car design.

The New Beetle has been accorded an overwhelmingly "good" rating in tests conducted by the Insurance Institute for Highway Safety, which have already resulted in some improvement to the model's safety features.

These are complementary but different to the testing undertaken by the federal New Car Assessment Program. For the latter evaluation, the full width of a car hits a rigid barrier at 35mph (56kph), a particularly demanding test of its restraint system.

By contrast, the Institute's work involves a 40mph (64kph) frontal offside crash intended to gauge the effectiveness of a car's front end structure, or crash zone.

CHANGES TO THE AIRBAG

As noted, the New Beetle has front and side driver and passenger airbags and dual locking shoulder belts. After

SAFETY FIRST

discussions between the IIHS and Volkswagen, and following an initial offset test, the company changed the size of the airbag vent hole. The Institute then undertook a second test as the design change was brought in during the introductory year, and the ratings that follow cover both tests.

As far as the car's structure and safety cage were concerned, the car achieved a good rating. It was found that there was minimal intrusion into the driver footwell area or rearward movement of the instrument panel.

DUMMY TESTS

The only measures not to be rated good by the Institute were the restraints and dummy kinematics, which were regarded as being "acceptable." In both tests the dummy's head bottomed out the airbag as the car rebounded from the barrier.

In the second test, the dummy's head brushed the window sill as it rebounded toward the driver's seat. Otherwise, the Institute considered that dummy movement was controlled "reasonably well."

Injury measures were judged to be good and again involved testing with dummies. The result of measurements taken from the neck, chest and both legs in the offset test indicated the low risk of injury. A high head acceleration occurred when the dummy's head struck the steering wheel in the first test, and was rated only as acceptable. But acceleration was low in the second test with the modified air bag.

IMPROVEMENTS ARE MADE

In its original form, the Institute found that the New Beetle's head restraints in cars made early in 1998 were poor when related to the average sized male. However, an improved version attained a "good" rating after better geometry was introduced in the middle of 1998. The Beetle was the only car, amongst 16 small models tested, to earn such a plaudit.

The restraints were high enough and close enough to the back of the average man's head to limit relative head and torso movement in rear-end collisions—the kind of movement that often causes whiplash injuries.

The performance of the car's bumpers was judged very good following four crash tests at 5mph (8kph). These are the sort of accidents that occur in congested traffic. There was no damage in the rear-into-flat barrier and rear-into-pole tests. Damage was minimal and amounted to just $134 worth following two front bumper flat and angle barrier tests.

The New Beetle was accorded a "good" overall evaluation. The IIHS judged that the driver space was maintained well in both frontal offset crash tests; measures in the first test indicated the possibility of minor head injury although the redesigned airbag in the second one reduced this risk.

The overall evaluation, when compared with other small cars, was "good" based on both tests.

Side airbags, belt crash tensioners, belt force limiters, and daytime running lights were all considered to be strong pluses in the ongoing quest to make cars safer.

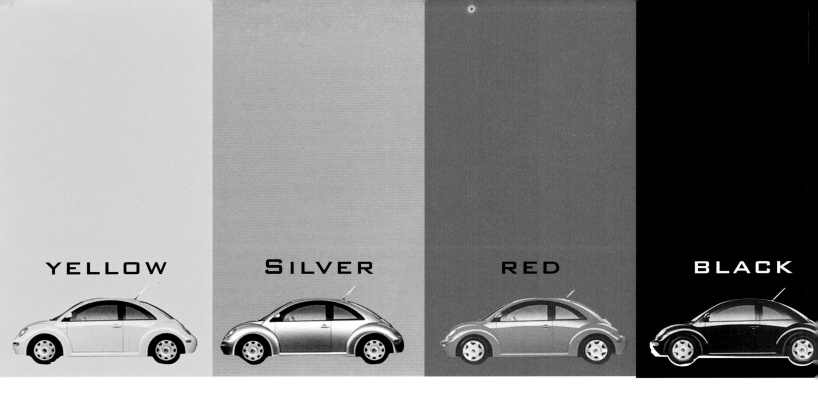

YELLOW　　SILVER　　RED　　BLACK

COLOR AND TRIM OPTIONS

WHEN HEINZ NORDHOFF launched the Export Beetle in 1949 it was available in just one color—blue-gray. He obviously thought that if Henry Ford could sell his Model T successfully in only one color, then there was no reason why he couldn't do the same!

Fortunately, things have gone a long way since then, and the New Beetle is available with a wide variety of color and trim options, a number of which were revealed to the public during the model's development from show car to production car.

The yellow option originally appeared on Concept 1, which also featured a black interior, while red was first used on the New Beetle Cabriolet at the '94 Geneva show.

A memorable black version of Concept 1 was unveiled at the '95 Tokyo show, which was where leather trim first appeared. The light brown coloring featured then is not one of the variations on offer, although we can be quite certain that such a material would never have been contemplated for the original no frills Beetle.

As can be seen, there are at present eight body colors available. The standard finishes are yellow, red, black, and white, with metallic paint offered on the dark and light blue, green, and silver versions.

In its standard form the New Beetle's interior is offered with a Primus velour seat fabric in a choice of cream, black, and gray color shades.

The cream, gray, and black partial leather variations are offered in the P2 package, while the leatherette versions, which carry the P3 designation, are available in a similar variety of hues.

Incidentally, when you buy a New Beetle, as an official extra you can choose a key chain with a colored plastic tag to match the finish of your car. They are accordingly available in black, blue, green, red, white, and yellow.

Of one thing we can be certain: if the original Beetle is anything to go by, these color variations are just the start.

Volkswagen's stylists won't have any shortage of inspiration when it comes to deciding new themes. When the New Beetle was launched at the '98 Detroit show there were no less than 882 concept drawings on display suggested by members of the public via the "Volkswagen of America" web site—customizing by computer, you might say!

WHITE BLUE LIGHT BLUE GREEN

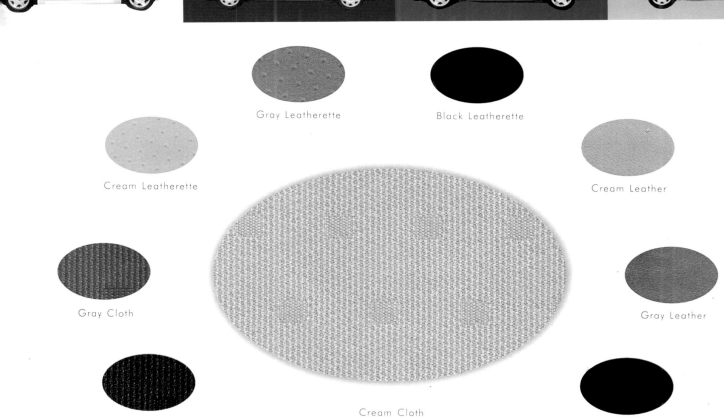

Gray Leatherette

Black Leatherette

Cream Leatherette

Cream Leather

Gray Cloth

Gray Leather

Black Cloth

Cream Cloth

Black Leather

1934 Germany's chancellor, Adolf Hitler, commissions Ferdinand Porsche to design a People's Car to sell for under RM1000 ($142).

1940 The first KdF-Wagen is built. Some 630 sedans and 13 cabriolet (open) cars are completed by 1944 but they go mostly to high ranking Nazis.

1937 Hitler decrees that the Volkswagen will henceforth be a state-funded project.

BEETLE TIMELINES

1939 The first stage of the car's factory at KdF-Stadt in northern Germany, some 50 miles (80km) east of Hanover, is completed.

1940 Manufacture of the KdF-Wagen-based Kübelwagen—Germany's equivalent of the Jeep—begins, and it remains in production throughout the war.

1938 The Stuttgart-based Porsche bureau completes the design of the renamed KdF-Wagen ("Strength through Joy" car) with its distinctive, cost conscious rear air cooled engine.

1945 With the ending of the war, the British army takes over the factory, its adjoining town is renamed Wolfsburg and the car reverts to the Volkswagen name.

1949 The Volkswagen company returns to German state control and Heinz Nordhoff, appointed by the British the previous year, continues as general manager.

1949 The factory-approved Karmann-built cabriolet version enters production. The model is the vanguard of updates and engine capacity increases.

1949 The first Volkswagen is exported to America, Nordhoff having initiated the creation of a better equipped Export model.

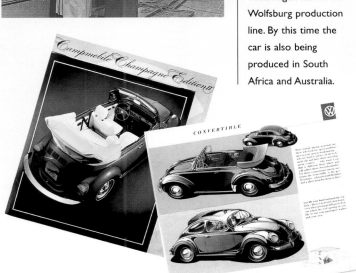

1955 The millionth Volkswagen leaves the Wolfsburg production line. By this time the car is also being produced in South Africa and Australia.

1955 Volkswagen of America Inc. is established in New York, although in 1962 it moves to Englewood Cliffs, New Jersey.

1955 The Volkswagen becomes America's best-selling foreign car with 28,907 examples sold representing 49 percent of automotive imports.

1957 Manufacture of the Beetle begins in Brazil and the São Paulo plant is destined to be the largest center of production outside Germany.

1964 Volkswagen de Mexico is established at Puebla and starts on the production of the original Beetle.

1968 With 423,008 buyers, US sales peak. Americans are calling the car the Bug, while the rest of the English-speaking world calls it the Beetle.

1969 Beetle worldwide production hits an all-time high when 1,291,612 cars are manufactured. Of these no less than 1,076,897 are built in Germany.

1977 VW withdraws the Beetle from the American market. It is replaced by the Golf, which is sold in the US under the Rabbit name.

1978 Production of the Beetle ceases in Germany although the cabriolet survives until 1980. Volkswagen's Mexican factory continues to supply the European market with sedans.

1974 Volkswagen announces the front-wheel-drive Ital Design-styled Golf hatchback. It has nothing in common with the Beetle apart from its wheelbase and is destined to be its successor.

1975 In America the Beetle is replaced as the US's top-selling import by the Japanese Toyota Corolla.

1972 Volkswagen announces, with 15,007,034 examples completed, that the Beetle has overhauled the Model T Ford as the world's best-selling car. Ford then "discovers" another 1.5 million Ts but this total is also overtaken by the Beetle in 1973.

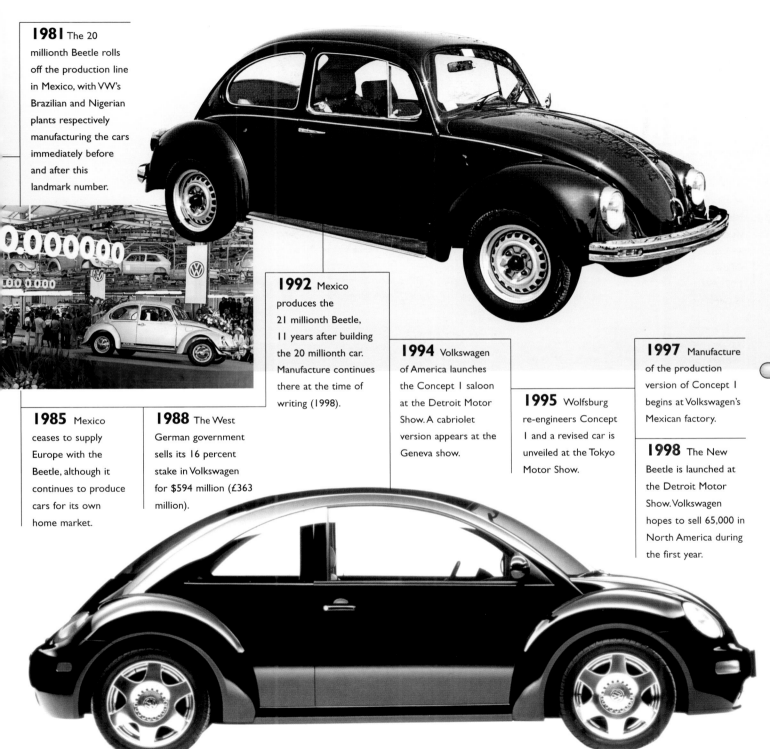

1981 The 20 millionth Beetle rolls off the production line in Mexico, with VW's Brazilian and Nigerian plants respectively manufacturing the cars immediately before and after this landmark number.

1992 Mexico produces the 21 millionth Beetle, 11 years after building the 20 millionth car. Manufacture continues there at the time of writing (1998).

1985 Mexico ceases to supply Europe with the Beetle, although it continues to produce cars for its own home market.

1988 The West German government sells its 16 percent stake in Volkswagen for $594 million (£363 million).

1994 Volkswagen of America launches the Concept 1 saloon at the Detroit Motor Show. A cabriolet version appears at the Geneva show.

1995 Wolfsburg re-engineers Concept 1 and a revised car is unveiled at the Tokyo Motor Show.

1997 Manufacture of the production version of Concept 1 begins at Volkswagen's Mexican factory.

1998 The New Beetle is launched at the Detroit Motor Show. Volkswagen hopes to sell 65,000 in North America during the first year.

Less flower.

> **" ...A SERIES OF DISARMINGLY HONEST BUT SIMPLE ADVERTISEMENTS THAT HAVE SINCE ENTERED THE REALMS OF ADVERTISING LEGEND.... "**

If you sold your soul in here's

IN 1959 VW EXECUTIVE Carl Hahn took over the running of Volkswagen of America. One of his many initiatives was to award the car account to a new advertising agency, the New York based Doyle Dane Bernbach. (The firm was commonly referred to simply by its initials, DDB.) It initiated a series of disarmingly honest but simple advertisements that have since entered the realm of advertising legend.

With the arrival of the New Beetle, Volkswagen decided to revive the concept, and the campaign includes such messages as "A car like this only comes round twice in a lifetime," "See what happens when you wish for the same thing," and "If you were really good in past life, you come back as something better." Potential New Beetle owners are invited to "Hug it? Drive it?" Perhaps some 30 years on these will become collectors' items—just like the originals.

Suddenly the world's glass is half full again.

Drivers wanted

The message is unambiguous and intended to strike a nostalgic chord with intending buyers—or their parents

More

Left

Although inspired by the originals, the new advertisements retain their own identity

Lime.

Right

A DDB original. Black and white photographs invariably featured

Lemon.

This Volkswagen missed the boat.

The chrome strip on the glove compartment is blemished and must be replaced. Chances are you wouldn't have noticed it; Inspector Kurt Kroner did.

There are 3,389 men at our Wolfsburg factory with only one job: to inspect Volkswagens at each stage of production. (3000 Volkswagens are produced daily; there are more inspectors than cars.)

Every shock absorber is tested (spot checking won't do), every windshield is scanned. Volkswagens have been rejected for surface scratches barely visible to the eye.

Final inspection is really something! VW inspectors run each car off the line onto the Funktionsprüfstand (car test stand), tote up 189 check points, gun ahead to the automatic brake stand, and say "no" to one VW out of fifty. This preoccupation with detail means the VW lasts longer and requires less maintenance, by and large, than other cars. (It also means a used VW depreciates less than any other car.)

Volkswagen plucks the lemons; you get the plums.

Drivers wanted. Ⓥ

the 80s
your chance to buy it back.

The New Beetle's distinctive profile evokes memories of the original

Drivers wanted. Ⓥ

power.

Index

CREDITS AND ACKNOWLEDGMENTS

EDITORIAL DIRECTOR

Will Steeds

ART DIRECTOR

Philip Chidlow

DESIGNER

Allan Mole

DESIGN SUPPORT

Justina Leitão
John O'Hara

PHOTOGRAPHY ART DIRECTION

Roger Hyde

EDITOR

Simon Tuite

PRODUCTION

Neil Randles

PICTURE CREDITS

Key: t = top; b = bottom; c = center;
l = left; r = right

CHAPTER 1

1 John Alflatt/Quadrillion Publishing; *2/3* Andrew Dee/Quadrillion Publishing; *4 & 5 (tl & tr)* John Alflatt/Quadrillion Publishing; *10/11* Volkswagen; *12/13* Volkswagen; *14 (tl)* Volkswagen; *14/15 (bc)* Audi; *15 (tl)* John Alflatt/Quadrillion Publishing *15 (tr)*; Volkswagen *16/17 (t and inset)* Volkswagen/Keith Seume Collection; *16 (bl)* Volkswagen; *16/17 (b)* Volkswagen; *18 (tl)* Rodney Rascona/Volkswagen; *18/19* Tim Andrew/**Car** magazine; *19 (tl & c)* Rodney Rascona/Volkswagen; *20* Volkswagen; *21 (tl & c)* Tim Andrew/**Car** magazine; *21 (r)* Volkswagen; *22 (tl)* Volkswagen; *22 (br)* **Car** magazine; *23* Volkswagen.

CHAPTER 2

24/25 Andrew Dee/Quadrillion Publishing; *26 (tl)* Keith Seume Collection; *26 (bc & br)* John Alflatt/Quadrillion Publishing; *27* Keith Seume Collection; *28* Volkswagen/Keith Seume Collection; *29 (bl)* Volkswagen/Keith Seume Collection; *29 (tr, cr & br)* Volkswagen; *30/31* John Alflatt/Quadrillion Publishing; *31* John Alflatt/Quadrillion Publishing; *32/33* Andrew Dee/Quadrillion Publishing; *34/35* Don Eiler/Quadrillion Publishing; *36 (tr)* Volkswagen; *36 (bl)* Don Eiler/Quadrillion Publishing; *37* John Alflatt/Quadrillion Publishing; *38* John Alflatt/Quadrillion Publishing; *39* Andrew Dee/Quadrillion Publishing; *40 (tr)* Don Eiler/Quadrillion Publishing; *40 (bl)* Andrew Dee/Quadrillion Publishing; *41* Andrew Dee/Quadrillion Publishing.

CHAPTER 3

42/43 Andrew Dee/Quadrillion Publishing; *44* Volkswagen; *45* Alex Puczyniec/**Car** magazine; *46/47* Volkswagen; *48* Richard Newton/**Car** magazine; *49 (tr)* Volkswagen; *49 (br)* John Alflatt/QuadrillionPublishing; *50* Glenn Paulina/**Car** magazine; *51* John Alflatt/Quadrillion Publishing; *52/53* Volkswagen; *54/55* Volkswagen; *56/57* auto motor and sport; *58* Glenn Paulina/**Car** magazine; *59 (l)* Glenn Paulina/**Car** magazine; *59 (tr)* Volkswagen; *59 (br)* **Autocar**;

60 (tr) auto motor and sport; *61* Glenn Paulina/**Car** magazine; *62 (tr)* Les Bidrawn; *62 (cr)* auto motor and sport; *62 (br)* Don Eiler/Quadrillion Publishing; *63* Ian Kuah; *64* Don Eiler/Quadrillion Publishing; *65* Volkswagen.

APPENDIX

66 Volkswagen; *67* John Alflatt/Quadrillion Publishing; *68* John Alflatt/Quadrillion Publishing; *69* Andrew Dee/Quadrillion Publishing; *70* Volkswagen; *71* Volkswagen.

TIMELINES

72 (tl) Author's collection; *72 (cl, bl & tc)* Keith Seume Collection; *72/73 (t)* Keith Seume Collection; *72/73 (b)* Author's collection; *73 (tr, cl, c & cr)* Author's collection; *73 (bl & bc)* Keith Seume Collection; *74 (tl & cl)* Keith Seume Collection; *74 (tc, cr & br)* Author's collection; *75 (cl)* Keith Seume Collection; *75 (tr & br)* Author's collection.

ADVERTISING

76/77 Volkswagen; *77 (tc)* Keith Seume Collection.

Acknowledgments

Many thanks to the following for their help: John York, Pat Trulove and Chris Moore at Hawthorne Imports, 9001 Broad Street, Richmond, Virginia; Cynthia Tate and the International Volkswagen Association; the National Motor Museum, Beaulieu; the public relations staff at Volkswagen of America, Germany and the UK; Michael D. Daniels, Regina Lyell and Bobby Price in the US and Luke Theochari in the UK for allowing their cars to be photographed; Derek Copson (indexing); Kathie Gill (proof reading); Ian Kuah and Philip de Ste Croix (Americanizing); Kay Rowley (picture research) and Robin Wager.